Lost @ 30,000 Feet

Lost @ 30,000 Feet

A Business Leader's Guide to Understanding & Navigating the Complicated Digital Business Growth Landscape.

By **Dave Conklin**

Founder & CEO of Conklin Media

Published in the United States by Conklin Media, a division of Conklin
Web Properties, LLC, Quarryville, Pennsylvania.

Also published as an ebook in 2020
Under ISBN 978-0-578-57806-4

Print Version
ISBN 978-0-578-57805-7

Printed in the United States of America on acid-free paper

www.lostat30k.com

To Jodi, for believing in me and supporting me while getting so little recognition for our successes.

Everything I do, I still hope impresses you.
(I even rewrote this ten times)

To Dad, for always encouraging me to just go do "it."
As if "it" was never a big deal.

To Mom, for creating my confidence and being my biggest role model.

TABLE OF CONTENTS

"Ignorance Can Give the Lost One A Sense of Catastrophic False Confidence."

-Dave Conklin

FOREWORD

By Ryan Deiss, Founder & CEO, DigitalMarketer.com

Boy, do I wish I'd had a book like this when I started on this strange journey.

Digital marketing. It's one of those phrases that means everything to some CEOs and nothing to others. Again and again, it confuses the heck out of the business world. Here's the thing: it's not the phrase's fault. The onus to get with the program and with the times is on business leaders. I've said as much and taught as much for 20 years now. ***Dave Conklin understands this better than most.***

Like myself, Dave is a veteran of the digital marketing world. We both started working in that young, evolving industry back in the late-1990's. We hustled. We learned everything we could on our own and with other like-minded early tech adopters about how to market using emerging technologies. We built niche sites that made people money. We started to figure it out.

Things change. You don't have to tell that to the generations who have grown up with the Internet at their disposal. The tech changes. The social media channels shift. The ways to reach out to customers adapt. The ways to tag, track, and redirect traffic back to generate leads morphs.

Dave has seen and lived those changes—heck, like me, he's still living them. And beyond living them, Dave is sharing them, which I'd argue is even more important. Because, you see, one thing that hasn't changed is that all across the business world CEOs and C-Suite types at companies of all shapes and sizes are still, as Dave says, "Lost @ 30,000 Feet," when it comes to both what digital marketing really is and how to effectively use it.

Dave and his vibrant, informative book, which you luckily now have before you, is seeking to change that. It's well past time that CEOs got their heads out of the clouds when it comes to digital marketing. It's time to really learn how to provide ground support for their companies, build proper digital marketing teams, support and empower those teams to perform effective campaigns, and start seeing social media for what it really is: the most powerful marketing channel in existence today. It's time that every business leader learned how to digitally market versus tossing around and stumbling over what's become a bit of a catchphrase.

We all get a little lost at times. These days I've become world famous through my work with my company, DigitalMarketer. We do everything we can to teach others how to effectively, you guessed it, market digitally, whether that means deciphering the often-misunderstood fields of search engine optimization, content marketing, sales funnels, or email marketing, just to name a few.

But that wasn't always the case. I remember being a college kid at the University of Texas at Austin in the late 1990's watching the Dot-Com boom grow without me. I knew I wanted in. I just wasn't entirely sure how yet. Now I teach marketers how to be great marketers. Marketers like my colleague Dave Conklin, who, with this book, has taken it upon his shoulders to continue teaching, training, and pulling CEOs out of the clouds.

I hope you'll follow his lead. If you do, your company, and the fantastic digital marketing staff you'll build and empower, will thank you many times over.

-- Ryan Deiss, Founder and CEO
www.DigitalMarketer.com

INTRODUCTION

First off, I have to say I'm extremely humbled that you picked up this book. I've spent years of my life trudging, digging, finding new clients, cold calling, selling and traveling. I've done just about everything to figure out how I could become the absolute best of the best in my industry. Along the way, I never really talked about my efforts, not in the marketing sector at least. I never went out on stage at a marketing-focused events and said, "Hey, look at me!" while pounding my chest. I have, instead, focused on creating a large resume filled with business success stories from all over the globe; businesses whose bottom line revenues I've helped grow. Now things are changing. I'm here to share these stories and my knowledge with you. It's an exciting time for me, and I'm truly honored that you've decided to join me on this journey.

As you'll soon learn, I'm passionate about helping business leaders who have been so focused on the big picture that they got lost while helping their teams navigate "on the ground". Here's an example of the "C-Suite to ground" disconnect I see again and again. Every leader is expected to understand how their customer service teams should properly handle customer's concerns on the phone. Why, then, do so many CEOs laugh about how "Tweets," "Snapchats," and "Facebook messages" are things they know nothing about and have zero to little interest in becoming familiar with. The truth is that *their customers are communicating* through those channels. Talk about a blind spot. Talk about a missed opportunity. My goal in these pages is to unpack just that, along with other similar C-Suite failings in the name of building the best brand and company you can, in a world that is increasingly dependent on digital marketing and communications.

THE PERSONAL SIDE

While this is a book on business growth and business navigation, I'm not a "business celebrity." Unless you've seen me speak, you probably have no idea who I am. If we're going to take this journey together, it seems we should know a little bit about each other, so I'd like to take a moment here to share some personal details about myself and my family before we dig in. If you don't care, feel free to skip to the next section — I won't be offended.

My name is Dave. I have an amazing wife, Jodi, who is my absolute rock and has supported me on the "back end," so to speak, through all the years of my career. It's not easy being married to an entrepreneur who always has a new idea, always wants to take a big fat loan out, and always wants to throw down on some huge risk in the name of doing something they think is new and magical. I'm so grateful that Jodi always believes in me, even when things are hard. As a matter of fact, when things have been hard, it almost seems like Jodi believes in me even more as she has continually put her full-blown trust in everything I've done.

I also have two sets of twins, and my kids are amazing. My daughter Emily works with me every single day, helping me build the business growth agency I'm currently involved in by serving our clients. She's incredibly bright and passionate about life. My other daughter, Haley, attends Penn State University and is a medic in the Air National Guard. Doing it all on her own, she has made her own path, her own way, and she should be pounding *her* chest right about now. My boys, Matt and Marc, are total rock stars. They are still in school so I have no idea what they're going to do with their lives yet, but I can't wait to see how it all happens.

THE BUSINESS SIDE

So, what about the work stuff?

Well, I started off in the real estate industry in the late '90s. I was young and achieved a tremendous amount of success quickly in about the most boring way possible: cold calling.

While selling newspapers at a young age, I'd learned that cold calling was pretty much the way to go. If I made enough cold calls, talked to enough people, and faced enough rejections, I knew I'd eventually get enough sales to earn a living on commissions. It was just a matter of working hard enough to hit the equation. So I sat in my little office and opened up the blue phone book. You probably haven't heard of the blue phone book. It was basically a reverse phone directory like you can find online today. Using the book, I could look up specific phone numbers based on their street address. I was able to call every single house on any street. So I drove around my area and found properties that were really expensive. I wrote down the street names. I wrote down the cities. Then I came back and looked up those street names and called every single house. "Smile-and-Dial" for the win became my way.

To this day, I still use cold calling in every business I run. I encourage my clients to do the same. As you can imagine, it doesn't always get the greatest response. It gets even worse when I talk about how we have programs to track, report, and measure the efficiency and success of each and every rep involved in a cold calling campaign.

I have learned, however, that the truly remarkable employees, the "A-players," actually love the software we use. Human beings are inherently lazy. Generally, as a species, we don't want to be held fully accountable for our actions. However, the top 2 percent of people, those above-mentioned "A-players" love being held accountable if it means they're going to experience more success.

Why can't we all be 2 percenters all the time?

When thinking of 2 percenters, I'm reminded of my current and former business partners. I have always intentionally placed myself around talented people. The people I've had strong business relationships with are the reason I'm *even* able to write a book like this. It's through these people that I've come to understand that if you want to be a true entrepreneur, and not just a person with a *job*, then you can't do it by yourself. As I write this very sentence, my business partners: Matt, Josh, and Steve are working out details on a recent client acquisition we are involved with while my team handles the details.

None of the work I do, or this book, would be possible without being surrounded by amazing people. Before we get any deeper, I'll thank you all here. Josh and Matt, for being who you are as humans, and as professionals. Steve and Steve (yes, there are more than one), Patrick, Rory, and Randy – thank you for being with me all those years where we learned, were challenged, and had a great time, and thank you to those of you who continue to look forward to the future together with me.

Finally, thank you to the hundreds of people who have worked on my teams, even those of you who may not have agreed with my decisions. Every single relationship shapes who we become, and I'm grateful for the seasons I have had with each of you.

THE GOALS FOR THIS BOOK

Let me start off by saying this isn't a book with specific detailed tutorials on implementing marketing campaigns. This is a book for the C-Level executive. It's for business owners and leaders of organizations with marketing teams. It's for C-Level marketing leaders and marketing directors. It's for people whose world focuses on leading marketing teams and organizations.

This is important. Trust me. I've had so many CEOs and business owners look at me and say, "it's not my job to be in the weeds." That's one of the statements that drive me insane. Today, when most CEOs don't understand something, when they just don't *get* it, they get upset and frustrated because they feel out of control. They scramble to surround themselves with people who they *believe* know how to fix the problem. They start interviewing and hiring people for a position they don't even understand themselves—not because they aren't lost in the weeds, but because they haven't even looked to see what's in the weeds.

I don't expect CEOs to be in the weeds pulling and plucking, but I do find it irresponsible that so many business leaders seem perfectly content not even knowing what the weeds are, let alone the solutions to the problems in the weeds. Think of it this way: while a doctor is the person who addresses a medical problem (a ground-level issue "in the weeds"), how many CEOs would allow an operation to happen on their body without understanding what was going on? Not many, I bet.

23

Doesn't it seem a bit ridiculous then that someone would feel comfortable running an organization without even comprehending how to begin fixing the problems it's having?

Sadly, people often decide to avoid certain knowledge when it comes to tech and marketing, because they feel "out of control" in those areas. It's time to change that pattern. Not knowing what you don't know is a common challenge we'll seek to overcome. Many of the tools we'll go over within this book will give you competitive intelligence into what your competitors are doing. This intelligence is unlike anything we've ever seen in business. It's possible, today, to literally peer inside your competitors' growth campaigns to see how they are structured and know exactly what they're doing. You can, even to some degree, see the results they're getting.

I meet with CEOs all the time—through meetings like Vistage International, Leadership Conferences, and in actual boardrooms—as I travel. After speaking with them, these executives often respond with this almost magical look of appreciation. It's really wild. I've heard quotes like, "My gosh! I didn't even realize this stuff existed, and I don't know what the heck you just said—but I know that my company is not doing it, and my team has no idea how to do it. Do you have a card?"

I'm flattered when I hear this stuff. The frustration for me is that I've been having these same conversations in boardrooms now for 18 years. It's time for CEOs to stop sailing in the air at 30,000 feet while looking down at their businesses and having no idea what's on the ground.

I once saw a really interesting chart that breaks down the changes in advertising over the years. The reality is up until the mid-90s—even into the very early 2000s—business leaders understood marketing, and they were effective in leading their organizations because of it. They didn't necessarily understand how the printing press worked that printed the direct mail piece they would later be sending potential customers. But they certainly understood there were data-list companies out there with consumer data they could purchase, allowing them to know who to send direct mail to. They certainly understood the idea of bulk mail. They certainly understood that a certain type of direct mail piece would have a higher conversion rate than another. And they also understood that those direct mail pieces could result in sales or people showing up at their location to buy stuff, and why.

I could easily go through analogies in the areas of billboard advertising, television, radio, etc. All business leaders accept the idea that there are potential customers watching, listening, and viewing just about everywhere. The idea that certain television stations or shows would have a better demographic for a business's audience is understood as well. The same goes with radio and billboard. It's not a new idea. Just about every CEO understands the importance of starting with your demographic in mind and making sure you're visible to that group in order to raise awareness about your company's products and/or services.

In the early 2000s, though, technology started to change what CEOs understood. The reality is that unless you were born after 1985, you probably don't see communication tools like Facebook, Instagram, or Snapchat as communication tools at all. You probably see them more as "fads" or "toys."

But these communication channels can actually increase the revenue of a business. In fact they do *just that* every single day for companies that realize what they are and actually engage on those channels properly. Most business leaders are completely clueless when it comes to social media, and I'm not saying this from my armchair. I talk to at least 10 new CEOs every single week on conference calls who want our agency to get involved and help their business to grow. My team and I coach them through the "weeds," showing examples of what's been done by other companies, and how they can achieve the same results.

I feel like it's time for CEOs to understand all of this themselves, so they can properly empower their marketing teams and do something about this huge disconnect. This book is designed to do just that.

My goal is to get this book in the hands of as many CEOs as possible across the country. Not to make money—there's little money in books, unless you're Brian Tracy or Stephen King—but to share this message so that they'll actually understand how this digital marketing thing works. They need to know what they should expect from their teams; how to hire marketing talent properly; and how people are communicating today through social media and different technologies that simply didn't exist even five years ago, in some cases.

I hope you're as excited as I am. I'm pretty brash. I'm pretty blunt. And while you're going to feel like you're getting into the weeds a little bit, especially if you have no knowledge of this stuff at all, I'm asking you to trust me. The conversation we're going to have will be fun, thought provoking, and challenging.

But I promise you—I absolutely promise you—that if you read through this in detail you'll be a better leader of your company. So let's get started.

IT'S JUST A NETWORKING EVENT

One of my absolute favorite ways to describe digital marketing to people who are in a state of confusion is to compare the web to a networking event. Bear with me here. Start by looking at the Internet— Facebook and Twitter and Snapchat and all of these different sources all over the Web—as buildings. The "links" that you click on to go from one site to another are basically roads and highways where you can quickly move from location to location. If you go to the LinkedIn building, inside you'll find thousands of events. At these events, individuals with common interests are communicating and sharing information they care about. This information is often regarding their work or their companies. There's often an open invitation for you or your team to join in those conversations.

Facebook is the same way. If you drive down the road to the Facebook building and go inside, you'll see rooms that people have rented. These would be Facebook pages or groups where you have people sharing ideas with others who have common interests. Twitter is the same way. You have hashtags there, where people can post about something that has to do with a specific idea. You can then click on a hash tag and see tweets about that same idea. So not only is the internet a series of buildings with rooms and groups and gatherings, it's also a place where you're able to instantly create your own building and pull multiple groups from multiple locations into one spot all together.

It's a really fascinating thing when you think about it. Sales teams that see the internet this way are able to do some amazing things with the information. Never before in the history of business in our world has there been so much transparency around what people do, what their needs are, and how they prefer to communicate. The problem for most business owners is they only see the advertising side of these things.

For example, a typical business leader who sells orthodontic equipment will see there's a forum on a website where people who work in the orthodontics industry are communicating. They'll say to their sales reps, "Hey go to this forum and sell our stuff. Put some links on the forum that point to our website." So the links go up. And guess what happens? Forum moderators immediately delete them because they offer no value to the conversation. After that, the business owner and the sales reps decide that interacting on forums simply doesn't produce ROI.

One of the first things that I like to talk about is how important valuable and share-worthy content is to potential customers who can grow your business. Very few business leaders provide their marketing teams with adequate budgets for legit content creation. By legit content creation, I don't mean a blog or an article. I mean something truly unique, different, and inspiring to the people who are checking it out. Content that *actually* adds value to the lives of those who see it.

To dig deeper, let's say there's a networking event at a local chamber of commerce meeting and a lot of my potential customers are going to be there. Of course I'd arm myself with some business cards. But if I went to that networking event, walked up to those people, and pushed those business cards into their chest saying, "Here's my card. Call me if you need me," it would obviously be an instant turnoff to every single person there. Imagine a sales rep running around from person to person just pushing their cards at people and offering no value whatsoever. It's asinine, right? It's a waste of time and resources, and a risk to one's reputation—kind of like spamming an internet forum.

Now let's say that rep has an actual solution to someone's problem. Maybe the rep did some online research and found out that one of the individuals who would be attending the networking event was having a challenge with a certain issue. The sales rep then does a write up on exactly how the solutions their business provides would solve the prospective problem. They do this write up in a helpful way where the potential customer can see the actual value and the solution to the problem. They don't talk about price at all. Now when the rep walks up to that prospect and says, "Hey, I noticed that you had this challenge. Here's a solution to your problem that I wrote up for you," that person is going to be so much more responsive and open to collaboration.

The Internet is exactly the same way, whether it's an email that you're interrupting someone with, or an ad on Facebook. It gives you an opportunity to present solutions to the problems of potential customers.

Most often, when marketing to a cold audience, ads on Facebook shouldn't sell your stuff unless there's a massive discount that would be impossible to ignore. The typical, lame, 25 percent discount that everyone does isn't worthy of a cold Facebook ad unless you have a $10,000 product. Don't do that with your advertising online. Instead, create something really cool that helps to solve a common problem. Then put the ad out there about that specific tool or resource. After you have people seeing and/or using that resource, you'll have the opportunity to offer your product to them in ads. Build your audience and create some credibility for yourself, *then* sell.

Creating content doesn't just mean writing articles. It doesn't mean posting on social media. Creating content means creating valuable tools and resources online that aren't available anywhere else. This could be compiling a bunch of different resources that exist out there into one good resource. Or it might mean creating infographics that solve a common challenge that isn't clearly explained anywhere else.

The book you're reading right now is valuable content (I hope). I'm not going to make a million dollars. I'm probably not even going to make a hundred thousand dollars on this book. The time I'm investing into this book, from a selfish angle, is so that you read the book and then understand that I actually know what I'm talking about. Then, maybe you call me to get involved in your business in some way, or use one of my products. That's the selfish business focus of why I'm creating this very content that you're reading right now. But it has to be valuable to you or to growing your organization, or else I just look like a buffoon.

So now you might be asking, "Where do I start?" Your website, in this world of networking events, is your home. It's your building that you get to control. If done right, your website should be your absolute greatest employee. It's a non-sleeping entity you can direct real people to 24 hours a day, seven days a week. It's always there to showcase what you're able to do for the world. Heck, people can be listening and watching videos from you or your team, which convert leads into buying products while you're sleeping. Beyond being open *all the time*, it's quite affordable. Sadly, most businesses don't value their website like an employee, and therefore fail to invest in it.

Let's pretend you were in the market to make a purchasing decision—hiring a lawn care company, for instance. If you're driving down the road and you see a building that has weeds growing outside with a "Lawn Services" sign, would you trust that company? Of course not. Your website is your online storefront and place of conversion. It should be your best employee and best present your company.

In 1980, none of this could have happened. To get your brochure in someone's hands they had to physically see you or receive it in the mail, which was really expensive. You couldn't put testimonial videos inside of a brochure. You weren't able to carry an interactive experience where you asked someone questions and got feedback without being there. There is so much available today that's not being taken advantage of by businesses. It blows my mind.

I can't stress it enough—treat your website as your greatest employee. Look at the Internet as a networking event. See the social networks and search engines as buildings that people go to search out information and communicate about common interests.

A quick note about search engines and their part in all of this: search engines are like libraries where people go and have the world's information right there. It's free to walk over and grab it. Imagine again when someone goes to the lawn care section (and you are a lawn care provider), being able to see that that person is seeking out lawn care and then making sure your book is right there in front of them. It's a huge opportunity, and you just have to take advantage of it. So many people don't because they've had bad experiences in the past, which typically comes from not hiring the right people.

A QUICK NOTE ABOUT ROI

We are about to get into some details in the next few chapters. These chapters won't be talking specifically about return on investment from spends in the areas we're discussing. I want to assure you, however, that every single thing you do in your business from a digital communication or digital marketing perspective is trackable to a dollar. Companies are implementing creative ways to track things you would have never imagined were even trackable. You just have to have the right players on your team who understand how to make this happen.

Any marketer worth his or her salt will be able to show you ROI, or lack thereof. One of the things we love to do internally is build landing pages and send paid search traffic to those pages. We don't do this to make money, but to find out what keyword phrases actually drive the highest profit per visitor. If we understand what keywords will make us money, we can make really important decisions on how to guide our search engine optimization in the future.

My point: everything is trackable. Everything is measurable. ROI is literally the only reason you would even do anything we're about to get into.

Later on in the book, I will be going over measuring ROI and specifically what you can expect from your team, in terms of reports - and the tools they can use to get them.

SOLUTION BASED VS. INTERRUPTION MARKETING

In future chapters we're going to be looking in depth at how each individual social network, search engine, email marketing platform, display ad network, and affiliate program can benefit your company. Right now, though, I need to make sure you understand the difference between solution-based marketing and interruption marketing.

THE DIFFERENCE

Interruption marketing sounds bad to some, but it shouldn't. Remember what we talked about previously. It's imperative that your marketing offers value to the people who see it. So, interrupting someone with a highly valuable ad is acceptable because it's so valuable.

In a solution based marketing campaign, your content is going to provide a solution to a query the prospect placed in a search engine or in Facebook or another platform. But it all starts with a search where they're looking for something. On the interruption side, you can still find people who have specific needs and desires. The interruption-based model, model, however, looks at what someone has previously looked up online, what they're currently looking at now, or a specific thing about them, like their job title, for example. You then interrupt them with an ad that you know would be of interest based on your targeting. Here are a few examples of interruption marketing.

INTERRUPTION MARKETING EXAMPLES FROM DIFFERENT PLATFORMS

FACEBOOK

Let's say someone's on Facebook getting some updates on their grandkids—finding out what they've been up to, looking at pictures, etc. This person likes "Victorian Furniture Digest Online," data about them that Facebook shares with advertisers, like *you*. An advertiser knows their age, knows they like Victorian Furniture Digest Online, knows that they're a female, and knows that they have been searching in the previous few days about new love seats. As they are scrolling through Facebook, an ad comes up for love seats that are Victorian in style. This is an interruption ad that could be extremely effective.

Another Example might be a movie trailer. Someone has liked the X-Men movie on Facebook. Advertisers are able to see that. When there's a new X-Men movie coming out, highlighting a specific 15-second clip of the trailer as a teaser that encourages them to click to watch the full trailer would be another example of Facebook interruption marketing.

INSTAGRAM

There's a local grooming company that does a really great job of interruption marketing. They know people who like animals in a certain geographical area based on what Facebook / Instagram and others share with advertisers. The grooming company has a really cute image of a dog that shows up on the Instagram feeds of those individuals who like pets. It's a really cute picture of a dog with the sudsy hair getting a bath. The text of the ad reads, "Is it time for your dog to get a bath?" That would be another example of interruption marketing.

LinkedIn

On LinkedIn, you can target people specifically based on their job title, the size of the company they work for, what college degree they have, where they've worked in the past, among other criteria. If you have a solution for people with a certain job title, in a certain industry, at a company of a specific size, interruption marketing on LinkedIn can be amazing because you can actually interrupt people. But you have to have very, very good content, which we'll talk about generating in a little bit.

Ad Networks (Display Ads on External Pages)

Interruption marketing can take place through display ad networks. You can have your ads run on pages around the web that are focused on specific topics and placed on specific websites, through Google AdWords (now called Google Ads), and other means. All of this is interruption marketing with banner ads.

Messaging Apps & Platforms

Messaging apps like WhatsApp and Facebook Messenger allow you to interrupt within a chat thread. Like it or not, these companies and chat methods can see what users are talking about within those ads and therefore, show ads based on the solutions to the problems that are being experienced by users.

EMAIL

Then there's email marketing. You can send emails to individuals, who again, similar to LinkedIn, have specific job titles and specific goals within their companies. Targeting these potential clients with email marketing can be very effective for starting relationships with people.

TWITTER

NOTE: Twitter has banned political advertising, which is mentioned in this section. However, the theory is still 100% applicable in most categories.

On Twitter, people will often post challenges that are having or opinions that they have. You can target people based on that with interruption marketing. For example, if someone has said on social media that they don't like a specific political candidate, many social platforms allow you to sell t-shirts or tchotchkes or whatever to support or not support a certain candidate. It can be a great way to raise funds. This doesn't just work for politics, but anything people are passionate about. In short, people often share their opinions in quick hits on Twitter, and then you can target them with ads based on specific things they've recently tweeted about. If someone says, "Man, my dishwasher broke again!", you can have "dishwasher" and "broke" as flagged keywords in Twitter and then interrupt them with ads for your dishwasher repair service or solutions for getting a new dishwasher.

SOLUTION BASED MARKETING EXAMPLES FROM DIFFERENT PLATFORMS

On the flip side, we have solution based marketing. Solution based marketing primarily rises from search engines.

YouTube

YouTube is actually a search engine. Believe it or not, people go there and they search for things all the time. If someone is searching for "how to repair my dryer," an advertiser (again, that's *you*) can have an ad come up before the video advertising your dryer repair services. This can be geo-targeted to cover certain locations as well.

You can also create great content (videos in this case) and optimize them to appear at the top of the video listings.

Search Engines

The search engines themselves are obviously, well, search engines, right? Think Google, Bing, Yahoo, and others. With solution based marketing, your goal is to make sure that when someone searches for a specific solution (and they're in a geographic area that makes sense for you) that you appear as a resource to solving their problem. This includes paid and organic social, which we'll get into in future chapters.

Business owners targeting prospects in a certain geographical area should always appear when someone is directly searching for a phrase indicating they're a potential customer. Which is so easy to do today compared to years past. The only challenge here is the cost. But if you have your business systems rockin' and rollin', investments should be covered quickly.

Those are the differences between solution based and interruption marketing. Almost everything we do fits one of those categories. Now once someone is digitally introduced to you—meaning they come to a landing page on your site, visit a specific tool, or download a specific thing—you should then interrupt them with retargeting.

You can use email, banner ad traffic, Instagram, Facebook, and many other tools to retarget them online with more interruption marketing. Interruption marketing is actually even more effective when it's done on the retargeting side than when it's done on the cold side. We're going to talk about that in a lot more detail in future chapters. From now on, when we talk about interrupting people or creating solutions, this is what we mean.

UNDERSTANDING CONVERSION PATHS & ROI

We've gone over how the Internet is really a gigantic networking event. We've talked about how you have an invitation to all of the different events happening within the larger event. We've talked about ROI and why and how all of the things we're going to be discussing in detail later always come back to ROI. We've also looked at solution based marketing versus interruption based marketing, and some of the platforms where you can utilize those types of marketing effectively.

Now I'd like to talk about understanding conversion paths and how it leads to return on investment. Most marketers at companies today are stretched too thin. They simply don't have the time to put together systems and plans that will provide the C-Level executives what they need to make strong marketing decisions. Every single website should have very clear stories and goals that are to be accomplished when traffic arrives. We're going to talk a lot more in the upcoming chapters about how to actually get the traffic to arrive there, but right now I want to focus for a moment on what happens when prospects are actually on the site.

First and foremost you have to backtrack your goals. If you're in a service based industry you probably want people to sign up for some type of consultation. In this consultation, it's likely you go over a needs analysis and determine specifically what you can provide the individual with that so that they'll give you moolah. If not a consultation, you may want them to fill out a form or send you an email.

To make this happen effectively, you're going to have to build some trust first. So many websites I see don't show examples of successes from clients, which are absolutely crucial to include in a service based industry. Testimonials from customers build an incredible amount of confidence, especially if they're on video. So much so that it has to be part of this conversion path. When a customer finds your website through solution based marketing (in other words through a search on Google, for example) they land on your site not having any kind of a relationship with you yet.

When this prospect lands on your site they need to start to go through a story. They have to clearly understand what exactly it is you do and what kind of a result they'll get from working with you. Then it needs to be extremely clear what it is you want them to do. Keep in mind that what you want them to do can't be overly aggressive in the beginning. As a business leader, this is where you need to arm your marketing team with the proper funding to create some amazing content. Again, amazing content doesn't mean a white paper that's surface level. For example, if you're in the washer and dryer business, have a piece of content on how someone could never have to worry about their washer or dryer breaking down again. Then provide an infographic on service and repair information, along with an option to then purchase that service from you.

Or consider the e-commerce industry. Having a product that's literally going to change the lives of the people who purchase it is huge. Even if it's just a basic product, you have to think outside the box. There has to be some kind of a challenge a customer is having that the product will solve. Or perhaps there's a recurring frustration with other related products in the industry and you're going to offer a way around that known headache. These could all be basic forms of content: free trial, demo, etc. Another example in the e-commerce world: reviews on the product. Video reviews of people using the product go a long way as solid content. But you have to get those customers viewing those videos involved in some way. Have they been able to download something? Or have you provided an online tool that benefits them in some way. Think about ways to offer your customers something fun and interactive that involves them with your website and also makes them like you more.

Understand that most people get an uncomfortable feeling in the pit of their stomach when they walk on to a used car lot and the salesman comes out from the building. This feeling, which is not a good one, really doesn't make a whole lot of sense. After all, the individual is coming out to help you accomplish what you want, which is to buy a car. However, human beings don't want to be *pushed* to buy that car.

"No, I'm just looking," is a typical thing people say when they walk into a store at the mall. In many cases, those people aren't just looking, though. They're actually there to make a purchase, or think about it at least. That purchase could likely be made more efficiently if they engaged with a salesperson. But for some reason, we don't want to have that conversation.

That's where creating great content that builds true value comes into play. First, you present the customer with something awesome that they want. Then it's time to take that offer to the next level, moving the client from this phase of awareness (they've landed on your site, which means they're aware) into the lead stage, which is where we get them to download some information, fill out a form, or call you. However, many people won't become a lead, and that's where retargeting comes into play. Once this person has landed on your website, your team can set up specific flags that will go off and put them on certain remarketing lists. For example, if a person was visiting the "tax planning" portion of your services page, you could have ads related to tax planning follow them around the internet.

Remember, though, that your ads have to be very similar to the page that they were on in order to make the connection and steer them back to you. If it's a product page your ads should certainly mention that product and show a picture of it. If your site displays a certain color scheme or visual appearance, you should make sure the ad matches. If there's a certain call to action on the page, you have to be sure that call to action also exists within the ads and pulls them back to the original page.

Let's recap. So we've gotten the traffic. We've made that audience aware of your brand and services; whether through solution based marketing or interruption marketing, they've landed on our site. Now we track the percentage of people who actually turn into a goal. A goal may be clicking through to another page of the website. Or a goal may be filling out a form. These goal funnels, or conversion paths, are crucial to monitor. They're like knobs you can turn up or down, improve, or split test. When we take this seriously, we can dramatically increase the percentage of people who land on our website and convert into actual goals, after which they become leads or are redirected into leads later.

But we still don't know who these people are. It's by finding out who they are (our next goal) that we move leads into prospects—people who have already downloaded a promotion, signed up for a coupon, or something similar. When these people receive information from you it has to be truly valuable. This download for them is kind of like the first date. If you look good to the prospect in your dating profile, but send them crappy content, they're going to come away with a very bad impression, which is good for no one.

Now that traffic is converting into leads, and leads are converting into prospects, of which you have contact info for, you'll be able to track the percentage of people from different sources that turn into leads, prospects, and then sales. You'll know where each lead, prospect, and sale comes from. If Facebook interruption ads are running, and people are coming to the page, and yet nobody is becoming a lead, then you know something's off.

Maybe, on the search side, you're advertising certain keywords and you find out that keyword "ABC" turns into a lead 60 percent of the time. Those leads turn into prospects 30 percent of the time. Then 20 percent of the time those prospects actually end up making a purchase. All of those things are trackable, but they have to be laid out in a flowchart so that your whole team can understand. You need to have your designers, your programmers, your writers, your ad managers in line. Everyone on the team needs to understand exactly what this conversion path is so they can measure it and effectively build new content, split test content, and make it better over time. They should then be reporting these charts to you from a high level so you can help make decisions with your experience and wisdom. Remember, one doesn't just wake up, run an ad campaign, and find it works. That's why conversion paths are so important.

If you're actually selling products online, you can also backtrack specific revenue numbers to specific channels and compare the ad spends so you can see you spent X dollars on Facebook. This can also be done through Pardot, Salesforce.com, and other enterprise-level solutions for service based industries and those that don't do e-commerce.

You'll be able to say, "We spent X dollars on Google Ads, Y dollars on LinkedIn, and Z dollars on retargeting. Here are the revenue numbers that came in from each channel."

After getting your initial metrics in place, your team should then create dashboards inside of Google Analytics or KissMetrics (or whoever it is you want to utilize) so they can show those high level reports to you. The paths get set up in flowcharts, and then the content is built around them.

You can actually track the phone calls as well, believe it or not. You can see what channels the phone calls came from, and what keywords people searched for that generated the call. We will go over this in more detail in future chapters.

Next, we're going to talk about the different methods of content that can convert well, which is really the foundation for your entire marketing campaign. You've probably heard it before. Content is king.

EMPOWER YOUR TEAM TO CREATE SHARE WORTHY CONTENT

(& What the Heck Share Worthy Means)

At the top of a chart I create for almost every marketing campaign, I put the phrase "share worthy content." Share worthy content is content that a certain demographic, whether it be people with a similar job title, age, gender, or other related demographics are interested in sharing.

Buzzsumo.com is one of the most amazing tools on the web for finding content examples that are "share worthy." BuzzSumo.com is a website you can visit and search for either a domain name or a keyword topic. It will show you content that has been shared socially on networks like LinkedIn, Facebook, and Twitter. This is a huge opportunity for you to find valuable content ideas that will spread.

Quick side note. I was once in a room with Jeff Hoffman, one of the founders of Priceline.com. We discussed the most important thing he does in his day to day that's made him a success. He shared with me an interesting idea (this is in his book, by the way). He reads, every single day, content that has nothing to do with the business he's in. He does this to find innovative things that haven't hit his industry yet. He can integrate, implement and execute these ideas, which then gives him an edge on his competition. It's the same with content. Finding content concepts that are sharing really well can help spur creativity and determine what might work well in your industry. So use buzzsumo.com to look up all kinds of stuff, even outside your industry.

The content you'll be creating can have a few different goals. One goal could be to have the content rank high in the search engines. To accomplish this, your team can create content that's focused on getting links from authoritative websites as we'll discuss in future chapters in depth. These links from authoritative websites heavily influence how Google ranks your website in the search engines.

Then we have social content goals. Social content is content meant to spread among a community. It could be a group on Facebook, LinkedIn, or Twitter. Social Content often needs to have a 100 percent non-promotional edge. If you start to talk about your business in a social piece of content, you'll basically be looked at as a spammer.

Many different companies have developed many different forms of content. Consider the entertainment angle. During political seasons, we have often photoshopped graphics of political candidates' faces on the bodies of people in popular TV shows or movies. Typically, this content was bipartisan, and because it was so newsworthy to two different groups of people and married two unlikely things together (a popular TV show like Walking Dead with candidates like Bernie Sanders and Donald Trump), it had a flair to it and spread rather quickly.

Then there's shock-and-awe content, where you're taking scary information and statistics and putting it into an infographic or video. With this content, you're showing a group of people something in a visual way they've never seen before. It creates that shock. So the entertainment end is humor, and the shock end is just that ... shock.

There's also interesting data-journalistic information. In data-journalism content, you take data that you find from multiple sources and combine it together, presenting shocking realities that may or may not be related.

Now the data science purists out there get frustrated with some of my data-journalistic content because it often doesn't go to the steps necessary to consider itself a proven theory. However, for the interest of conversation and getting data to spread, I see nothing wrong with creating some data journalistic content that doesn't actually have proof at the end, as long as you're indicating there could be more research done on a piece of content.

Here are a few examples. In the Houston, Texas market we linked data we found on the job safety ratings of chemical plants and then in oil refineries. We compared the two to determine which industry was safer. We then promoted this content to associations in the oil refinery and chemical industries. This content resulted in a lot of links. Another piece we did for an education website involved looking at the state-by-state college enrollment increases and decreases throughout the years in the United States. We created engaging maps and broke down increases and decreases. Comparing that information with state job data showed some very interesting content. If people are graduating often from a certain state and then the job unemployment rate decreases a few years later, it could be an indication that college degrees equal lower unemployment rates.

Infographics, if done well, are a great way to get content on the web that's extremely effective. The problem with infographics, however, is that so many people have gone the cheap route and done a "good enough" infographic, which ruins the idea of infographics for the rest of the infographic creators. This can be very frustrating to a high end marketer because it doesn't give the user an incredible amount of value.

If someone doesn't look at your content piece and go "wow that's awesome!" or "wow that was helpful!" or "wow that's hilarious!" or "wow that's shocking!" then that piece of content isn't good.

Calculators are currently a really great way to get content flowing as well. In addition to compiling resources in multiple areas, calculators are found all over the web. Furthermore, there are lots of great starting points like plugins that you can create rather easily. Some websites are made up of just calculators! The owners of these sites often use the calculators to generate leads.

You understand the difference between interruption marketing and solution based marketing. You understand how you need to look at having the traffic create a certain conversion on the site. We've talked about content that can be "share worthy" and content that can be used to create downloads and leads. It's now time to get into the meat and potatoes and actually talk about solution based traffic. Let's start by looking at discovering keyword phrases that actually turn into revenue.

RESEARCH : KNOWING WHAT YOUR POTENTIAL CUSTOMERS ARE SEARCHING FOR

As we've discussed, in digital marketing you're either interrupting someone during their private "surfing time" or you're becoming a resource in a search engine result when someone is actually looking for a product or service.

There's a huge benefit in knowing what people are actually searching for, and how that relates to your products and services. It's also important to note that many times there are situations where people are looking up things that would indicate they need your products or services, yet they're not actually searching for those specific products or services. One great example would be the real estate industry. It's very common when someone wants to sell their house that they look up their home's value first. I know this because I spent years in the real estate marketing world marketing to those very consumers. We made a lot of money through ranking in Google and other search engines for keyword phrases related to learning what one's home was worth. It would have been a lot more expensive to get the same traffic from a person who just typed in "best realtors in [city name]". Now I'm not suggesting that you don't want to rank for "best realtors in [city name]" if you are indeed a real estate agent. However, I want to make sure that you also understand that it's important not to ignore other opportunities out there.

So take a second and think about your industry. If you own or run a camping e-commerce website, think of things that people may be searching for in Google that would indicate that they have an interest in your potential products, but don't necessarily suggest that they're going to make the purchase right away. Today, we have tools like AdRoll, Google Ads retargeting, Facebook retargeting pixels, and many other methods that allow you to follow up with the customer once they hit your site. So it's not a completely lost cause if you generate search traffic from someone for a keyword phrase that indicates they have an interest but not an immediate desire to purchase.

Now don't get me wrong, some of those very specific keyword phrases can have incredible conversion rates. For example, if you have a $300 LED solar charging camping light (and by the way if none of those exist, I think it's a great idea and you should do it if you're in that industry) and someone is specifically typing into Google "best LED solar powered camping light," the conversion rate will be much higher than somebody typing in something like "coolest camping gear of the year."

So the big question for this chapter is, "what can we do to actually discover what these potential customers are searching for?" Before we even talk in depth, so many of the people I speak to at events around the country say, "Dave, look, I just don't think people are out there searching for our stuff. They're just not." For example, I was speaking with a person in the entertainment lighting industry. He provides lighting for events and shows. They are in a position where they feel like everyone already knows the people in that business and nobody's going to find them through search. We found something to the contrary in our research when looking up a couple of their competitors in some of the tools you can find at CEOKnow.com. You can also visit lostat30k.com for these links. This knowledge is easily available. No tech skills required.

We've discovered through the years, that there are a tremendous amount of financial opportunities available to those individuals who go out of their way to try and make sure that they are generating traffic for the keyword phrases that are entered into Google on a regular basis. So the first tool I want to make sure you're taking a look at (which, one last time, you can find at CEOKnow.com or lostat30k.com) is SEMRush.com. At the time of this writing there's a link for a free trial at CEOKnow.com for SEMRush. You can also use our tools directly at that site.

You can do one of four things with these tools.

First, you can enter your website. When you put your website into the tool, it will show you keyword phrases that your web site already ranks for in Google, but that you're not yet necessarily seeing traffic for.

So if you look at the data in the "POS" (which means "position") column in SEMRush after submitting your domain name, you'll see a list of keyword phrases. Then, after selecting to see the entire list of organic keyword phrases, you'll see phrases your site already ranks for in the top 10 pages of Google (top 100 rankings, as there are 10 results per page). Now, keep in mind, any keywords listed in positions 11 or higher aren't likely to be getting a whole lot of search engine traffic. This is simply because very few people go to the second page and beyond after doing a Google search. This is powerful information as it shows low-hanging fruit opportunities. As a leader of your organization, you can use this data to clearly drive your marketing team to perform activities that you can be confident will have quicker results.

You can also, as a CEO, look at the keyword phrases that your team is purchasing in Google. You'll find that information under the "paid keyword" area. This area can be enlightening. It's extremely common for companies not to use what are called "negative keywords" in their search ads campaigns. Typically, this happens when someone who's inexperienced in Google Ads is given a list of keyword phrases to "buy" in Google. They then send all the traffic to the home page and don't track anything. They spend a bunch of your money, yet can't show specifically how much revenue was generated from it. So the CEO gets frustrated and cuts the budget. They feel that PPC (also known as "pay per click", "search ads", or "Google Ads") "doesn't work for their business." Then they see me at an event and say, "Oh, yeah, we tried Google Ads, and it doesn't work for our industry."

Well, the reality is that they didn't actually do it right. It would be like going to a foot doctor to fix your ear. You probably went to a smart doctor, but she didn't have the understanding or ability to actually fix the problem you were having. A professional pie eater might be really good at eating pies but that's probably not the person you'd want to go to to learn how to bake pies, or even worse, go to to learn how to lose weight. You want to go to experts.

As an agency, I actually pay between $50 and $100 per hour to experts in the area of paid search. And the reason we pay that much is that these people are quick, efficient, have the experience, and understand how things work and don't work. They know how to convert, and they're experts in their field. Their results are night and day from what you'd get from a 23 year old with a college degree in digital marketing.

So you can look at the organic search rankings of your current site. You can look at the paid search rankings of your Web site and find keyword phrases that maybe you shouldn't be purchasing or that you need to add negatives for.

But **you can also look at your competitors' sites!** By going into this tool and clicking a button you can specifically see what those competitors are paying to rank for. You can see the ads they're running. And you can see what landing page they're sending that traffic to! This is the greatest competitive intelligence data that's been known to business since the history of business! Talk about a powerful tool.

Let's say there's a college that competes with the college you run, and it's your job to get more admissions. You can actually see, with this tool, exactly what keyword phrases the competing college is paying to rank in Google for, the ads they're running, and the landing pages they're sending that traffic to. You can then have your team recreate that same general campaign, with your look and feel and your psychology, knowing, in advance, that it's going to work! The competitor has already spent a ton of money and energy doing all the legwork for you.

What's crazy is the fact that such a tiny percentage of CEOs actually know this data even exists and is available. I can almost guarantee that less than 5 out of every 100 leaders I meet have even heard of these tools. It's because they're not empowering their marketing teams to purchase tools, not instructing them to how to utilize them (meaning what data will show key objective accomplishments), and simply not educating themselves on digital marketing.

There's yet another powerful thing you can do with these tools. Try looking up trade journal magazine websites that speak to your audience. When you do, look up the most popular phrases and pages of those sites. By doing so, you'll learn about your potential audience in a new way. You can then recreate and improve the resources you discover and publish them on your website. For example, internally, we're doing an infographic right now that breaks down how to lay out a website in a way that best converts traffic into calls and leads. We're spending a lot of money and time to make it really great so that it gets talked about on a lot of sites. We practice what we preach.

You see, the people looking up how to most effectively build a web page in a way that converts are the very people we want to talk to about becoming a customer. So we're going to provide value to them. We're going to allow them to download this infographic, which results in us being a thought leader in that area and leads to revenue down the road. This all starts with the research and keywords discussed here, and knowing, --instead of guessing, what your potential customers are searching for.

Once you've researched the keyword phrases you and your competitors are organically ranking for, the keyword phrases you and your competitors are paying to rank for, and the most popular pages on your site and the sites of others, it's time to do some research that starts with keywords rather than a domain. You can actually use the same tools. Instead of submitting a domain name, submit a keyword phrase. Let's use "Super Bowl party" as an example. When submitting "Super Bowl party" you'll find the phrase match list. You're going to see keywords like "Super Bowl party recipes," "Super Bowl party decorations," "Super Bowl party invitations," etc. You're going to see all these words added to the phrase you put in--"Super Bowl party." Now you may also find keyword phrases like, "super big chip bowl for my party," because it has the words "Super," "Bowl," and "party," in it. You have to make sure that you're keeping note of all those negative keyword phrases so that you don't end up purchasing those keyword phrases as well. Now, on the flip side, there's going to be something called related keywords. In the related keywords area, you will find keyword phrases that SEMRush, or the other keyword tools, find to be generally related to the keyword phrase you submitted. There are many other keyword tools available, but, as of this writing, we have found SEMRush to be one of the absolute best on the planet.

The takeaway: don't assume you know and understand what people are looking for in search engines, Amazon.com, or elsewhere. It's ridiculous to do so. You wake up every day, go to work, and think about things from within your business. You are in a bubble. In the end, making such assumptions is going to harm you and prevent you from knowing and understanding exactly what people are actually searching for. You don't want to be the person who assumes. We all know what assuming does.

SHOWING UP IN GOOGLE

I wrote about being in a bubble in the previous chapter, and I often suffer from this myself. I've been using the same acronyms for years, so it's very easy for me to get into a rut where I talk using phrases that business owners wouldn't necessarily understand. In the same way, business leaders sometimes speak using phrases that I don't understand. Vocabulary is huge.

With this in mind, I think it would be beneficial to quickly go over some of the phrases I'll be using here, so you have a clear understanding as to what I'm speaking about going forward.

The First one is "search engine optimization" or "SEO." This has two different meanings, really. Sometimes, when someone uses the phrase SEO or search engine optimization they are referring to the on-page text and technical factors behind a website. For example, the code that you may have seen that goes on behind the scenes to make a page look good (HTML, CSS, JavaScript, etc.). In some cases what is happening behind the scenes can be optimized for search engines, and it should be. However, there's a secondary part of SEO that many business owners don't even understand: "off-page" factors, which have, at the time of this writing, a higher impact on search engine rankings than the on-page factors.

Before we get into the off-page factors, let's cover a few items that are important when it comes to "on-page," without getting into the weeds, so to speak. To start, let's talk about ALT tags.

Each image on a web page has to have something called an ALT tag. This allows Google to understand what the image is about. It's also used when a visually impaired user is visiting a website. The ALT tag provides the user with a clear description, which can be read to them, as to what an image actually is. In your ALT tag, it's important to be very descriptive about what the image is and how it relates to the topic of your website or your web page. Google will use this information to understand why your web page is the best authority on its given topic.

Another thing to understand is the difference between a web page and a website. A website would be the collection of all of the different web pages that you can surf on your website. A web page would be referring to a specific page within that website. There are specific things from a technical perspective that need to be taken into account for both web pages and websites. While many of these things are overly technical, for the purposes of this book, a huge takeaway is that you need an expert for on-page SEO whenever you hire a design company. We have heard dozens of stories where a company spends $70,000 on a website redesign, and upon completion, they lose traffic, leads, and revenue. All of this happens because they hired a designer who wasn't an expert in SEO. This is talked about more in the Chapter, "A Geek Is Not A Geek."

Whenever you're setting up a site or modifying a site there are many on-page factors to consider. The most important are:

- Title tags
- Meta description tags
- H tags
- ALT tags

57

An on-page factor that's really important is internal linking. This is the strategy of linking the web pages within your website together in a specific way to inform Google what they are about and give them more authority about those topics. For example, let's say you sell widgets of different sizes and colors. You'd likely have a main internal page about the widgets you sell. You may then have specific pages about purple widgets, red widgets, large widgets, small widgets, and widgets in bulk. To internally link properly, you would ensure the main widgets page has links on it (you can click on the underlined words that are blue most of the time to travel to other destinations on the Internet) that point to each of those smaller, more specific pages. Those smaller pages should also link to the main page as well.

It can be helpful to picture each page of your site as a glass of water. With each quality link that points to a page, the higher the water gets in the glass. You don't want any empty glasses if possible. Some glasses are always going to have more water than others. On those pages, you can afford to pour water into pages that are empty. This leads to the most important search engine optimization factor: off-page links.

Google and the other search engines use *external* links from web pages outside your own site to determine relevancy and rankings. This gets into the off-page factors that have a huge impact on search engine rankings.

There's an exercise that I absolutely love to do, and I'm going to walk you through it now. Hop in front of a web browser if you don't mind. You can use your phone if it's handy or a computer or tablet. Go to Google.com and type the phrase "click here" into the search box. Then hit enter.

Just like with any search you would do in Google, you're going to see a bunch of websites listed. The one at the top that does *not* have the word "ad" next to it is the one that Google feels is the most relevant for the phrase "click here."

At the top, above the listings, it will say how many results there are now. This number changes all the time, but it's typically in the billions. I've seen it in the hundreds of millions as well. Either way, there's a lot of sites that Google has in its index that it finds relevant to the phrase "click here."

Now, keep in mind that Google is a robot, so to speak. It's a program (algorithm) that's making a decision as to which sites are the most relevant for the entered phrase. And it's showing those to you first. Both the order of this list and the pages Google lists in the first place, change regularly, as new website and web page information is discovered by Google's web spiders.

Look through the list, and you'll find some interesting things in the first 20 results (pages one and two if you have your search setting set to Google defaults). At the time of this writing, there's a link to the IRS's page where you can get your refund status. There's also a link to sign up for a PayPal account. Open those pages in a new window (click on them while holding the shift key).

Notice when you read through their content that neither one the pages have the phrase "click here" on them. Out of billions of results, you'd think the word click or the word here would be somewhere within the content of these top-ranking pages. If they're not, then why on earth do these pages and sites rank so well for the phrase "click here"?

This example has worked since I got into this business in the early 2000s. The reason these pages rank so high, and the reason that Google's algorithm feels they're so relevant to the phrase "click here" has absolutely nothing to do with the content on the page of those sites.

When people realize that the content on a site has little to do, in many cases, with the ranking position of a site for a keyword, the light bulb clicks on. The reason these pages rank so high is that there are so many web pages, all over the Internet, owned by all kinds of different people, that say things like "you're going to need to download Adobe Reader to read my PDF, So click here to download Adobe Reader." All of these links are what makes Adobe Reader's download page end up ranking in the top pages of Google, out of billions, for the phrase "click here."

There are other web pages that say "to check your IRS refund status, click here." And the underlined blue "click here" they click sends them off to the IRS.gov refund status Web page. The PayPal example is very similar. Someone takes PayPal for payments. They say "if you don't have PayPal, 'click here,' and you can set up an account for free."

This all shows us that a huge portion of Google's algorithm is based on external links that point to a website or a webpage. And those links build authority and trust in Google if they're from authoritative and trustworthy websites and it builds relevancy. If the links are on pages of content that are similar topically to the keywords being linked to, it's even better.

Now the other part of this, however, is the actual text on the page. We have a system we use (and have been using since I started in this business) called PowerPages. When Using the tools you learned about in the previous chapter (like SEMRush.com) we will put in a keyword phrase and export the list of phrases. We make sure to note all the phrases and build content around the relevant phrases in the list. It's very tedious, but we make sure that every single possible relevant word within that keyword phrase list is included in the content. For example, if the keyword was "home value," and another keyword was "home value report," and a third keyword phrase was "what's my home value," we would make sure that the words "home," "value," "report," "what's," and "my," all appear within the content we create for the site.

In order to build links properly, you have to have the assets we talked about a few chapters ago. It's so important to have content worth linking to. If you want a link from a relevant site, you have to create something awesome for their website visitors. If you don't, there's simply no reason for them to link to you.

USING PPC TO KNOW YOUR NUMBERS BEFORE YOU DO SEO

Ranking in the free area of Google, as mentioned above, is expensive to achieve. Creating content to build links to, optimizing that content, and then getting other sites to actually talk about that content can be extremely time consuming and pricey. However, the long game is well worth it.

The long term play on SEO is a great one *if* you know the money you're investing is actually going to pay off. Who wants to take the time and effort to do all of the work if you're not absolutely sure it'll return a positive ROI? Fortunately, there is a solution we've been using for more than a decade that achieves this goal.

Most people who think about PPC (pay per click search engine marketing) don't see it as a research and development tool. The truth is it's actually one of the best available tools for business leaders. To put it simply, why spend $5,000 per month for 10 months to get your site ranked at the top of the search engines, hoping that the traffic generated from those rankings will actually generate an ROI? Especially, when the alternative is to spend less than $1,000 *total* on traffic through PPC and measure the results, thus predicting what will happen later.

A REAL WORLD EXAMPLE

Rather than go through a bunch of theories, I want to share a scenario on exactly how I would suggest helping a client with this very thing.

To keep things simple, we'll use the example of a company that is interested in generating leads for their window treatment installation company. In other words, they want to meet people interested in window treatment installation services. We're going to specifically focus on "blind installation". They have never done any type of SEO before and have no data at all as to what would work.

The first thing I do in a situation like this is go to a tool called Ahrefs (Ahrefs.com) and use its keywords explorer tool. I don't want to assume that people are typing in the phrase that I think, so I start by simply entering in the word "window." Once presented with the data, I start looking for keywords and search volume (the number of times per month the phrase is searched for in Google). I want to find the main, high-level groups of phrases and to take note of them so I can build further research.

Here is what I see when I search for "window":

You'll see a number of keywords here that have nothing to do with blinds, and this is intentional. You'll also notice in this data that the tool found more than three million keywords that are searched for often and contain the word "window."

Now I'm going to go through and begin finding phrases that would indicate the searcher is looking for what I want to generate leads for. In this case, "window blinds."

I can quickly see the words "treatments," "blinds," and "shades" are all potential candidates.

This exercise will help you to learn about what people are searching for outside of what's in your head. It's incredibly important because *you* are the supplier, not the client. And consumers often don't know what they are looking for by "industry buzzwords" that may be common for you to use.

You really want to play with this tool at this stage and find at least five different "groups" of keywords. As I went through this, here is the data that I looked at:

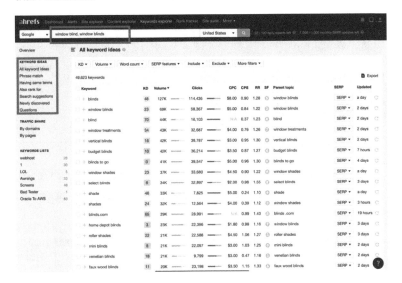

The boxes indicate what I typed in and looked through. When I'm explaining this at speaking events, I often get questions about what the data actually means. Let me explain. Here are the headings (many of the descriptions are taken directly from Ahrefs.com, unless I felt it would be helpful to add some context).

Keyword	KD	Volume ▼	Clicks	CPC	CPS	RR	SF	Parent topic	SERP	Updated
blinds	48	127K	114,436	$8.00	0.90	1.28		window blinds	SERP ▼	a day

Keyword is the actual keyword phrase that the rest of the data is about. This is a phrase that is entered into Google by someone.

KD means "keyword difficulty." This is rated on a scale from 0 – 100, with 100 being the most difficult to rank for and 0 being the easiest. This is calculated by considering the competitive landscape found in the list of sites that shows up when the keyword is searched for.

65

Volume is the total number of unique times per month the keyword is searched for in Google. In the case represented in the image, the phrase "blinds" is entered into Google about 127,000 times per month.

Clicks refer to the average monthly number of clicks on the search results that people make while searching for the target keyword. Some searches generate clicks on multiple results, while others might not end in any clicks at all. (This description was taken directly from Ahrefs.com).

CPC Cost Per Click (CPC) shows the average price that advertisers pay for a click on their ad in Google's paid search results for a target keyword.

CPS Clicks Per Search (or CPS) is the ratio of clicks to keyword search volume. It shows how many different search results get clicked, on average, when people search for the target keyword.

RR Return Rate is a relative value that indicates how often the same person searches for a given keyword over a 30-day period. Since it's a relative value, it doesn't show the exact number of repeated searches and should be used when comparing keywords against each other.

SF Search features are the different categories of data that shows when a given query is made to Google. They include:

1. Google Ads (AdWords) top
2. Site links
3. Image pack
4. Top stories
5. Thumbnails
6. People also ask
7. Google Ads (AdWords) bottom
8. Shopping results

Parent Topic is important because it shows you the "head term" that a phrase is associated with. These parent topics can be used to guide you in deciding the sections or main pages you'll want to create to do the testing we discuss below.

SERP means "search engine result page." Clicking on this for each keyword, you can see the data that was discovered by Ahrefs when doing their research.

Updated is the date when the data you're looking at was last analyzed and reported.

Okay, back to the data now.

The first few head terms I'm going to look at are window blinds, mini blinds, Venetian blinds, and faux wood blinds.

Take a look at the squares in the image below, and you'll have a better understanding why.

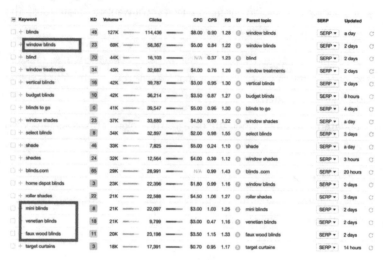

Keyword	KD	Volume ▼	Clicks	CPC	CPS	RR	SF	Parent topic	SERP	Updated	
+ blinds	48	127K	114,436	$8.00	0.90	1.28	◯	window blinds	SERP ▾	a day	↻
window blinds	23	69K	58,367	$5.00	0.84	1.22	◯	window blinds	SERP ▾	2 days	↻
+ blind	70	44K	16,103	N/A	0.37	1.23	◯	blind	SERP ▾	2 days	↻
+ window treatments	34	43K	32,687	$4.00	0.76	1.26	◯	window treatments	SERP ▾	2 days	↻
+ vertical blinds	16	42K	39,787	$3.00	0.95	1.30	◯	vertical blinds	SERP ▾	2 days	↻
+ budget blinds	10	42K	36,214	$3.50	0.87	1.27	◯	budget blinds	SERP ▾	8 hours	↻
+ blinds to go	0	41K	39,547	$5.00	0.96	1.30	◯	blinds to go	SERP ▾	4 days	↻
+ window shades	23	37K	33,680	$4.50	0.90	1.22	◯	window shades	SERP ▾	a day	↻
+ select blinds	8	34K	32,897	$2.00	0.98	1.55	◯	select blinds	SERP ▾	3 days	↻
+ shade	46	33K	7,825	$5.00	0.24	1.10	◯	shade	SERP ▾	a day	↻
+ shades	24	32K	12,564	$4.00	0.39	1.12	◯	window shades	SERP ▾	3 hours	↻
+ blinds.com	65	29K	28,991	N/A	0.99	1.43	◯	blinds .com	SERP ▾	20 hours	↻
+ home depot blinds	3	23K	22,396	$1.80	0.99	1.16	◯	window blinds	SERP ▾	3 days	↻
+ roller shades	22	21K	22,588	$4.50	1.06	1.27	◯	roller shades	SERP ▾	3 days	↻
mini blinds	8	21K	22,097	$3.00	1.03	1.25	◯	mini blinds	SERP ▾	2 days	↻
venetian blinds	18	21K	9,799	$3.00	0.47	1.16	◯	venetian blinds	SERP ▾	2 days	↻
faux wood blinds	11	20K	23,196	$3.50	1.15	1.33	◯	faux wood blinds	SERP ▾	2 days	↻
+ target curtains	3	18K	17,391	$0.70	0.95	1.17	◯	target curtains	SERP ▾	14 hours	↻

When diving into the head term "window blinds," we can see the keyword phrases that contain the word "window" and the word "blinds." Now, I don't want to eliminate the singular version of "blind," so that's why I entered "window blinds, window blind" into Ahrefs.

When I do this, I notice that many of the phrases are from people looking for retail locations, and I'm not really convinced that these individuals are looking for installs. So, out of curiosity, I researched "blind install." And *boom*. Here is our gold mine.

(PARDON THE INTERRUPTION) - THE IMPORTANCE OF SEARCH INTENT

We need to break from this keyword data for just a moment, because it's imperative that you also consider search intent when deciding what phrases to use PPC to test for. Let me explain.

If you're lazy and just purchase a bunch of keywords without thinking about the psychology of the searcher, you're going to waste a lot of money off the bat. This often leads to incredible discouragement about the effectiveness of search marketing. I have heard it hundreds of times throughout the years where a CEO approves a "test budget" to spend on paid search keywords. So, the marketer gives Google a list of words, they make some ads and run the campaign. And ...

It. Doesn't. Work.

Why?

Because no negative phrases and/or words were added - and more importantly, the psychology (search intent) of the searcher wasn't considered.

One of the best examples I can think of to show this in the "real world" comes from a time where my company was spending about $30,000 per month on phrases related to "home value."

We advertised the phrase "home value" as well as the phrase "house value," in addition to all of the long tails for each.

The home value keyword phrases had a MUCH higher conversion rate and quality than the house value keywords, and we had no idea why. But we're talking 10%+ better, so we wanted to understand why.

We separated people who used the word "home" vs "house" in their searches and discovered something crazy, but so obvious. You see, when most people refer to the place they live, they call it a home. But when they are referring to someone else's home, they refer to it as a house.

At that time, the business we're talking about generated revenue by helping people who were thinking of selling their home, so we really wanted to talk to people who wanted to know what THEIR home was worth, as that's a strong indicator that they are thinking of selling their house (home ... haha).

Because people who are thinking of their home, refer to it as a home, and would typically type phrases including the word "home" rather than "house."

We were able to spend significantly more money on ranking for those keywords than we were the house value related words. We would have had no idea if we didn't have proper tracking setup.

This all goes to say that when you launch a paid search campaign, be sure to put yourself in the position of the users doing the search and think deeply about why they just typed in that phrase. It can feel great to see your site ranking in the search engines for phrases you believe people are searching for … but it won't matter to your bank account if you don't actually rank for the "right stuff." Cue (NKOTB).

Now, back to the blind installation example. After keyword research comes an important piece of the puzzle: the landing page.

THE LANDING PAGE

We have discovered a list of keywords relating to the phrase "blind install" that we know we can upload to Google and "purchase" on a per-click basis.

We now need to have a place for those people to land on our website that is custom tailored to them and their needs (see the search intent box above). In the beginning, I always recommend looking at some of the pages that other people are marketing, to get some ideas about what you should have on this landing page. However, a few years ago I put together an infographic that, at the time of this writing, had some best practices on what to include in a landing page.

You can find the post here:

https://lostat30k.com/landing-page

Don't be a lazy bum and send the traffic to your home page. When I'm doing audits for CEOs that's one of the things that absolutely drives me insane. We have, over and over again, increased revenue for companies by 20 to 30 percent simply by making a landing page and moving paid traffic there from the home page.

At the very minimum, you should have a trackable phone number on your landing page through CallRail, or another trackable phone provider. Also, be sure to include a form where people can request a quote or more information.

We also suggest a chat box. There are providers of live chat services that, if trained properly, do a great job at generating leads (you can check out our recommendations at LostAt30k.com).

Below you'll find an infographic we did a while back that breaks down what we have found to be important aspects of a landing page. After that, is the article we did on our blog breaking it all down.

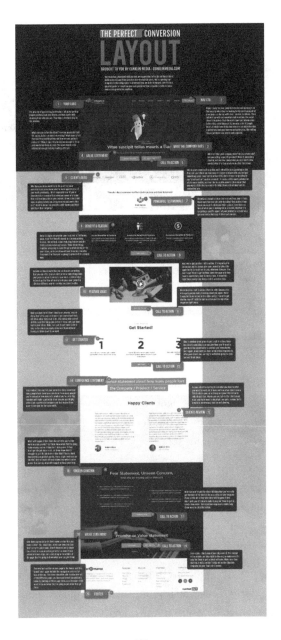

SECTION ONE

The first section is easily the most important—it only takes 10 seconds for a web page to make a good impression, or else the visitor will bounce for "greener pastures." That means the page your visitor's see immediately has to answer a lot of their questions:

- Who are you?
- What do you do?
- Why should the visitor care?

And it has to answer these questions quickly and coherently. But if you structure the layout in the right way, you can accomplish all this while simultaneously laying the groundwork for a conversion. Just use the right elements in the right spots.

1. **Your Logo.** The upper-left hand corner is prime web design real estate because that's where most of your visitors will look first. In Western cultures, we're trained to read left-to-right and top-to-bottom, so our eyes instinctively go here first. That's the perfect place to introduce yourself.

Additionally, it's a common web design pattern to have your logo link back to the starting page, so if your reader ever gets lost, most will click the upper-left logo to return to the home section.

2. **Navigation Menu with CTA**. Another common web design pattern is to have the navigation menu written across the top header. A lot of your visitors will expect this to orient themselves. You want to list all your important web pages so that visitors who already know where they want to go won't waste any time.

The most important part is the call to action, preferably highlighted in a different, contrasting color or separated as a button. This works best at the far right to punctuate the navigation menu. Your visitor's eyes will linger at the end of the line, so the right corner is ideal for a CTA.

3. **What Your Company Does**. Let's get down to business. You only have a line or two to explain succinctly what your company does (remember the 10-second time limit), so stick to the basics. There's time to elaborate later, but for now stay general with an overview. Your visitor just needs to know what you do and what industry you're in.

4. **Value Statement**. Here's where you explain why you're the best choice and why your visitors should care about you. Try addressing their specific pain points and demonstrating your competitive edge. Again, you only have a line or two, so be brief. A catchy, memorable slogan doesn't hurt, either.

5. **Call to Action**. Now that your visitors know what your company is about, throw out a couple CTAs as suggestions for how to proceed on your site. Think of the first section as your hook and these CTAs as reeling them in. A lot of your visitors will want more information about you, so add a link to tutorial videos or more written explanations. It doesn't hurt to include an option for your main closer, either.

As in the navigation menu CTA, you want these to stand out visually by using a contrasting color or separating them in a button. Don't be timid about the wording either. State clearly what you'd like them to do without being pushy.

Your CTA here—and on every other occurrence on the page—should always include an objection response. This is a short line pre-empting any objections visitors might have to sign up, such as mentioning that it's free or reassuring them that you won't share their email address.

Section Two

Here's where you add the information that's still important, but not as essential as the first-section fundamentals. Showing social proof can be a powerful sales tool, so do it here to make a good impression early.

6. **Client Logos**. A logo is worth a thousand words. Rather than saying "we've worked with them," show their logos instead. Not only are your past clients' logos instantly recognizable by your viewers, this format also saves screen space. The convention is to use a light gray color for the logos; it's easy to follow and there's no need to waste space explaining "these are our previous clients."

7. **Powerful Testimonials**. Include one or two of your best testimonials to elaborate on how your past clients appreciate your work. Visitors might be wary of what you say about yourself, so using the words of someone in their shoes, often holds more weight.

Most of your old clients will be happy to help. When requesting testimonials, don't be afraid to specify what aspects of your work you'd like them to mention. And don't forget to include the image, name, and job title of the speaker to make them seem more real.

Because we want to conserve space at the top, these testimonials should be short and sweet. There's another area below for longer, more detailed reviews.

SECTION THREE

With the main elements out of the way, we can start getting into specifics about what you offer and mention the peripheral benefits of your service.

8. **Benefits and Features**. Here you show three specific benefits or features you offer. To help communicate them visually, use representative icons above the text.

What features you mention, and in which order, also matters. We recommend this setup:

- Your first benefit should be about making or saving money. (That's what most visitors are looking for anyway.)
- Your second benefit should be about saving time.
- Your third benefit should be about relieving stress.

Accompany each benefit with a short description about how you provide it or why it's useful.

9. **Call to Action**. Repetition is a classic sales strategy that dates back long before the internet. You'll want to repeat your CTAs throughout

your web page, first to create a rhythmic reminder as your visitor scrolls down, and second, to make sure that they never have to search for a way to contact you no matter where on the page they are.

Section Four

It's best to include a video at the halfway point to keep your page visually stimulating and break up the monotony of text.

10. **Feature Video**. People all have different ways to process information. Some prefer text, others images, and yet others videos. By now you've covered the first two, and the halfway point is a great place for a video, both to satisfy visitors who prefer videos and as a way to break up the flow of content.

The actual content of the video is flexible. It could be a sample of previous work you've done, a video summation of everything you've already discussed above, or even a behind-the-scenes look at your process.

11. **Call to Action**. In case your video convinced your visitors to convert, include another CTA right below to remind them that you're just a click away.

SECTION FIVE

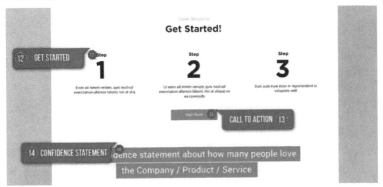

We're past the halfway point. Now we're free to discuss the finer details of what you do and how to present the information that appeals to some—but not all—of your visitors.

12. **Get Started (Steps)**. A certain type of visitor will want to know what to expect when working with you before signing up. For them, clearly list out the process in three steps—even if there are more than three steps, try to boil it down to three so it's easier to explain. The key here is simple: you want to explain enough to pique their curiosity, but not enough to make them think too hard.

13. **Call to Action**. Again, you want to add another CTA here to net the visitors who are convinced after seeing the step-by-step process.

14. **Confidence Statement**. Here's the ideal place to show an impressive statistic about yourself. Set the text apart in larger or flashier type to make sure it's noticed. Typically, the confidence statement covers:

- How many people you've helped
- How many products you've sold
- How much money you've made yourself or others

Big numbers here work well in conveying your skill or prowess, but mentioning awards or distinctions have the same effect.

SECTION SIX

As we near the bottom, we have ample room to display the longer versions of testimonials and client reviews.

15. **Client Reviews**. Here's where you show the full-quote testimonials from your clients. These have the same effect as product reviews, as visitors are more inclined to trust people just like them. These reviews should answer visitors' questions about working with you and erase any doubts.

As before, to humanize the speaker, include a picture of them, their name, and their job title.

Section Seven

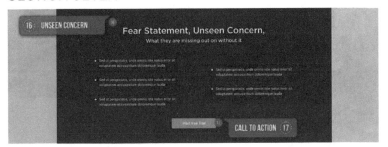

Winding down your pitch, explain what happens if the visitors don't hire you.

16. **Unseen Concern**. Otherwise known as the "fear statement," this area should play into the sales tactic of pain avoidance. In a bulleted list, show the visitors what they'd miss out on:

- They'd fail to get a job done
- The job would get done with less quality
- The job would take too long
- The job would cause them too much anguish

Keep these consequence points short—a single sentence or less—and round out the list to five.

17. **Call to Action**. Here's a call to action for the people convinced by the unseen concerns. You can change the wording or link location to match the problems you just outlined.

Section Eight

Finally, we get to the end of the page. Now it's time for your final closer and the footer to anchor the page.

18. **Value Statement**. Just like in the first section, you want to explain your value clearly: why you are the best choice. This is doubly important here; visitors scroll to the bottom of the page for many different reasons—they get lost, they want to see how long the page is, they're looking for something in particular, they prefer the navigation menu in the footer—and you want to make sure they see your company's main benefits no matter what.

19. **Call to Action**. Include your final CTAs here, again to guarantee the people who scroll to the bottom of the page see them. Like your initial CTA, you can include multiple options. And don't forget the objection response.

20. **Footer**. The last thing to appear on your web page should be your footer. Traditionally, this includes a more detailed navigation system, listing out the links and pages you don't have space for in the top navigation menu.

This is also a good place to include secondary information, such as reiterating your contact information, your office address, and your social media links. You can even elaborate a little more on your company, as well as throw in your legal text to cover all your bases.

We hope that you find a ton of value here, and that by implementing these items into your site that you see zillions of leads and duodecillions in revenue!

So, that's the article. It's helped many businesses by bringing some clarity to landing pages. As you work with your design team, use this as a guide and a checklist to make sure that any page your sending traffic to has these elements, and I can assure you that your landing page conversions will increase.

OFFER SOME VALUE WITH A LEAD MAGNET
(THANKS, DIGITALMARKETER.COM FOR THAT TERM)

In many cases, offering something of value to a visitor can be a great way to get them to do two things. First, it entices them to give you their contact information. Second, if you're offering the "right thing," it will clearly show their intent.

If you're providing a PDF titled "The Ultimate Guide To Hiring the Right Blind Installation Company Without Flushing Money Down the Drain," (not saying that's the greatest of ideas), you can logically assume that those downloading that guide are interested in having someone install their blinds. If they weren't, why would they download it?

You've got a list of phrases people search for. You've got a landing page. Now it's time to write some ads.

CREATING THE "WRITE" ADS

Again, please don't be lazy here. With many of the things we are talking about in this book, you can simply perform some Google searches and quickly discover what people are doing. While seeing what others are doing doesn't guarantee success, it certainly does give you a starting point.

If you're using tools like SpyFu, you can even see how long an advertiser has been running the same ad text. This is huge, of course, because if they continue to do it month after month, there is a great chance that it's working for them. When I speak at CEO leadership events I almost always ask the question, "If you saw the same billboard at the same spot on a highway for three years in a row, it's probably working, right?"

The answer to this question is, "Yes. It's probably working." Unless someone signed a really bad contract or just has a lot of money to blow.

The same goes for ads online. If you see them month after month, they are probably working.

With all of this in mind, here is what I'm seeing right now when I search Google for "blind installation.

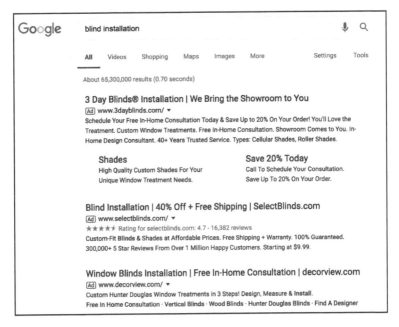

There are three ads there. Side note, currently there is a map listing below these ads, which we'll talk about later in the book.

You want to pull consistencies out of these ads to determine what you think you can offer. For example, the first and the third ads are less focused on the discount and more focused on "bringing the showroom to you" and "in-home consultations." The other ad (the second one) appears to be more of a discount-focused ad.

If it were me, I would look at the landing pages they are sending the traffic to and find the one that most aligns with my business model.

In the next chapter, we're going to be getting deeper into competitive intelligence, and we'll actually break down how to dig into these businesses even more to get data to launch with.

If there are multiple ideas that will work for your business model, consider running them all and doing a split test. In Ahrefs, we saw the approximate cost per click for each keyword phrase. So, when I'm thinking about clicks and costs on a new campaign, I tend to assume I'm going to be able to convert around 10 percent of the traffic to some kind of a lead. If I'm able to really target well, that percentage will go up. We'll get into that in later chapters when we talk about the advanced side of paid traffic.

From our research, it looks like we'll be able to get clicks for about $6 each:

Keyword	KD	Volume ▼	Clicks	CPC
☐ + blind installation	3	800	694	$6.00

This means, we'll be able to get a solid lead for $60. If we close 50 percent of those leads, we're at about $120 per sale.

Of course, in the beginning, this is all a guess. We can start to have more intelligent planning and budgeting conversations about this once we actually have traffic coming in. But if you're not hitting somewhere close to these numbers, there are definitely areas you can improve on.

And remember, the point of this particular exercise isn't even to make money on the PPC ads: it's to help us determine what keywords to focus on with our SEO efforts from the previous chapter.

Finding keywords that don't make money is a good thing, not a bad thing. We will know what phrases to eliminate from our SEO efforts, which is the point. Kind of reminds me of Thomas Edison's quote, "I have not failed. I've just found 10,000 ways that didn't work." With hope, you'll find some keywords that work well before you hit 10,000.

ADDING NEGATIVES

When I started using Paid Search, it was 2002. At that time, there wasn't such a thing as "negative keywords."

Now, however, as you see traffic come in, Google shares with you exactly what these visitors type into Google in order to get your ad to come up. There are many different ways to "buy keywords" in Google, including broad match, modified broad match, exact match, and phrase match. We're not getting into these until later advanced chapters, but it's important to understand in the beginning that if you buy the phrase "blind installation," and put no other limitations on it, Google will decide if it feels your ad should also come up for searches it feels are related, like "window decor," for example.

I always recommend using modified broad in the beginning. The way you do this is by simply adding a plus sign to each word. So, in purchasing "blind installation," one would enter into Google ads the following phrase:

+blind +installation

This tells Google that you want to be there only when someone has included the words "blind" and "installation" in their search query. Keep in mind, however, that this doesn't exclude everything else (which is why we're going to be adding negatives in a moment).

+blind +installation will also have your ad come up when someone searches: "best water softener installation companies for the blind." When you tell Google you want your ad to appear when someone uses the modified broad match bidding strategy, you're telling Google that as long as a phrase contains the individual words you entered, you want to market for it. This can work really well to make sure you hit all the potential phrases that some *may* enter. Just use it with that knowledge.

Once you see the actual phrases people are entering to see your ad, you can add negative keywords to your campaign. In the example we gave above--"best water softener installation companies for the blind"--we could add a negative for the word water. This would eliminate anyone searching for a water softener. However, that doesn't really fix the core challenge that's more likely to come up over and over again--people who are searching for things "for the blind."

Our solution for this is to add a negative for the phrase "for the blind." Once you do that, your ad will no longer appear for any search query that contains the phrase "for the blind."

OTHER MATCH TYPES

Match types work for both keywords you bid on as well as negative keywords you don't wish to appear for. Make sure you think deeply about what each selection you make communicates to Google, so you don't (a) waste a lot of money and (b) end up not bidding on anything because your negatives are too broad.

EXACT MATCH BID TYPE

Exact match is your ticket if you want to rank for the phrase "blind installation" with no words before, after, or in between the words "blind" and "installation." In some cases, when we are testing a keyword phrase list for a client, we will upload a list of exact match phrases.

This gives you a very accurate representation of what phrases will convert and not convert. Remember, this chapter is specifically about just that: finding out what keywords will convert so we know clearly what to go after with our long-term SEO strategy.

When uploading a keyword list, brackets surrounding the exact phrases communicate your desire for the bidding strategy to be an exact match. Consider the following:

- [blind installation]

PHRASE MATCH BID TYPE

Let's say you want to appear for anything searched in Google that includes the phrase "blind installation" within it, but also includes words before or after. Examples would be "affordable blind installation," or "blind installation in Dallas, Texas." If this is your goal, phrase match is the solution.

To achieve this, use quotes to communicate your desires to Google:

- "Blind installation"

BROAD MATCH BID TYPE

This bidding strategy is the one that will generate the most traffic by far. However, you run the risk of much of that traffic being irrelevant, because Google will decide if it feels terms are similar. So, if you tell Google you want to bid on "purple shoes," Google's algorithm may also show your ad when someone types in "lavender sandals."

There are cases we have seen where this strategy is beneficial, especially as a test to find phrases that you may not have thought of. However, if you deploy a broad match strategy, watch it like a hawk or you could waste a lot of money very quickly.

MODIFIED BROAD MATCH BID TYPE

My personal favorite, and the one I walked you through earlier is "modified broad." This is where you're telling Google that if a phrase contains all of the words, in any order, you want to have your ad shown.

This is a safe way to learn. But again, you could be limited by your own "bubble." We often live in a world where we have a common vocabulary with our peers, while our potential clients refer to us very differently when they're looking for our products and/or services.

MIXING AND MATCHING BID TYPES

You can also mix and match. Using the "purple shoes" example above, you could bid on:

- purple +shoes

This would allow Google to substitute the word purple, but only show the ad when the word shoes was searched for. So, your ad would be shown when users searched for "purple shoes," "lavender shoes," "plum shoes," etc.

You could also do things like:

- +blind installation [in dallas]

As an exercise, think about some keyword phrases that your ad would show for with that example. Modified Broad "+blind," broad "installation," and the phrase "in dallas."

TRACKING THE RESULTS

Before you start sending traffic to your landing page, it's really important to have tracking set up. We go into all of this in great detail later, but I know there are some over-achievers who are likely to run a campaign immediately after reading this chapter. So, at a minimum, here's what you want to do (again, we go into this in depth later, but here are the high level basics):

- Get a Hotjar account and install the code on your site (or, have someone on your team do it). Then, enable recording of the page you're going to be sending traffic to.
- Make sure you have that CallRail account we talked about earlier. Install the code and have it replace your number whenever someone comes from paid search with the trackable number.
- Install Google Analytics on the site. Then, link CallRail with Analytics, so when someone calls you, it logs as a goal in Analytics. I also separate first time calls from future calls. In most campaigns, those first time calls are incredibly important.
  - Be sure to enable all of the advanced analytics features.
  - Create a thank you that people see when after they become a "lead."
  - Set this page up in Analytics so that any time someone lands on it, it logs a "goal."
- Create a Facebook ads account and add the retargeting pixel to all pages of your site. This will enable you to retarget people later that have hit specific pages.
- If you're in B2B or think you'll be advertising through LinkedIn in the future, create a LinkedIn ads account and add that pixel as well.
- Create your Google Ads account, and link it with your Google Analytics account. Pull all of the goals you created earlier into your ad account. This will link up your ad spend to your goals

and give you a tremendous amount of information to work with.

Now it's time to hit the "go button." Whenever I start a new campaign, I watch real time analytics for the first few days closely. It's always fascinating to see the traffic come in, then check out Hotjar to see what they are actually doing on the site.

THE COMPETITIVE INTELLIGENCE GOLD MINE

Imagine if you could literally peer inside the minds of the most brilliant and successful marketers in your industry. Marketers who have successfully grown the businesses of your most profitable competitors. Imagine if you could get through the guesswork and just start with what you're sure would be a successful campaign.

Oh wait ... you can.

When I was doing high-level consulting with a large digital marketing company for a few years, we had a business leadership event where the entire theme was 'how to use what others have done to build your own profit center'.

The great thing (some would say the scary thing) about this is that you can see everything your competitors are doing. You can see the ads on Facebook that work for them, the content pieces they are promoting on Instagram that are bringing them revenue, and the pages of their site that are getting linked to from the "linkerati." (Thanks to Rand Fishkin for the term).

With this data in mind, you have an incredible starting point for your team to begin campaigns. You simply don't need to waste money on "testing" and "trying" without any guidance; it's all there for you. Let's get into what you can specifically do with tools like Ahrefs, SEMRush, SpyFu, and more.

AHREFS.COM

Ahrefs has data on keywords (which we went over in the last chapter), as well as sites (and a lot more; but these are the primary data points).

When you click on the site explorer tab, you can specifically see the keyword phrases that the site is ranking for and what pages of the site are the most popular in terms of how much traffic they receive.

Imagine you're getting into the business of selling knives. You're not sure which type of knife will be the most popular seller, though. You could simply enter one of the top knife e-commerce sites into this tool and see which of their products is the most popular. This is an incredible data point to understand. No need for focus groups!

In addition, you can look at the social section of the tool and see how the site is getting social attention. Maybe they had a contest or some kind of project that got an incredible amount of attention. You could create a similar contest or project and actually see who it is that may promote it. Once again, imagine tens of thousands of dollars in potential wasted money saved just because you had the data right in front of you.

SEMRUSH.COM

SEMRush gives you the opportunity to see the ads that your competitors are running to sell their product and services. We talked about this a lot earlier, so I don't want to repeat a lot of myself here, but this is one of most powerful tools out there and they have a great library of "how to" videos where you can learn more about using it.

SPYFU.COM

SpyFu also gives you access to the past. This tool lets you learn what ads people were running consistently month after month. If the company is paying month after month to run the same ads in Google, you have a pretty good data point that the ads are working effectively. You can even see the landing pages that they are sending the traffic to. There it is. Instant campaign.

A FEW SUCCESSFUL GRAY STRATEGIES

THE "RULES" WORLDVIEW

I have a worldview on "rules" that I'll likely write about in detail in a blog post in the future sometime. I was standing in an Apple Store in Lancaster, Pennsylvania with my assistant in 2019 when the idea came to me. Understand, I'm always trying to figure people out. One of the most common things I find myself searching for is the reason why some people feel they are capable of greatness and others simply don't. I've debated with myself if it's desire, faith in themselves, faith in something greater, laziness, or something else.

In my Apple Store "light bulb moment," the theory came to me that a part of it involves an individual's concept of "rules."

Picture, if you would a horizontal line. Well, no need to picture it.

Here's one:

Okay. The line above represents "rules." These could be rules that have been put into existence by society, business, religion, or personal experiences.

I believe that some people are born "beneath the rules." This means they figuratively look "up" at the rules from below. These people see rules as a ceiling in which society, and they need to stay under. They will often operate there for their entire life - and in most areas of their lives.

To be clear, I'm in no way suggesting these people are "wrong." They are often very happy and find life to be rewarding because they have clear expectations. If they achieve those expectations, they're good to go.

Here's another illustration for you:

On the other side of the conversation, there are people who naturally see the "rules" as a floor that's supposed to be built upon.

They see rules as a platform and go through life trying to create new ones. They automatically feel they have the "authority" to create these new ways of doing things.

With that being said, I'm on the side of the fence where I think that innovation requires the establishment of new rules and ideas using the rules of the past. Therefore, I often find myself looking down at the rules.

The ideas you're going to find here might be considered "sketchy" or "irresponsible" to some, and "innovative" and "incredible" to others. I'm not suggesting you do all of these things in your business's growth plan, but I am suggesting that understanding the possibilities can help you to do things that will greatly transform your business.

RANKING HYPER FOCUSED RESOURCE SITES

As discussed in depth above, one of the highest ROI ways to generate leads for your business or sales of your products / services online is ranking in the organic or "free" area of search engines.

Unfortunately, as it's such a lucrative way to generate revenue for your business, it's also one of the most sought after, competitive, and therefore expensive methods. To be effective, you need to do something to set yourself apart from your competitors, to Google, and other search engines.

One of these strategies is to create an SEO focused microsite geared to a very specific keyword phrase, or group of similar keyword phrases. A site that contains resources, guides, and content geared very specifically to helping the searcher find the information he or she needs. A site that gives them confidence that they've found their answer.

I'm often asked why this can't simply be done on the company's website. It's a great question, and the answer is simply that Google will reward sites that are laser focused on specific topics. A lot of examples are under an NDA, but my team and I have created many of these sites--in many different industries with great success.

One example is a company that was in a specific industry that wanted to rank for phrases like, "top _____ firms," "Best _____ firms," etc. We knew that it was going to be incredibly challenging for this company to rank for those phrases on its corporate website. To start, there was no previous content on those topics on the existing site. Additionally, Google isn't going to want to seem impartial. If someone searches Google for "Best _____ firm," and a specific company shows up at the top, Google looks like it's giving a recommendation and Google isn't in the recommendation business (well, at least not openly).

So we bought a domain called "top_____firms.com," and started creating content comparing different companies in that industry, profiling them, etc. We then gave these rated companies badges they could place on their site with links to their profile pages on our new domain.

This content combined with these links put the site at the top of the search engines extremely quickly. Just a few months later, our new site was ranking for a large percentage of the keywords phrases they were going after. It's also important to note that this site continues to rank to this day for those keywords and is still generating revenue.

Here are two charts showing this power.

Their corporate site (top) vs the microsite (bottom):

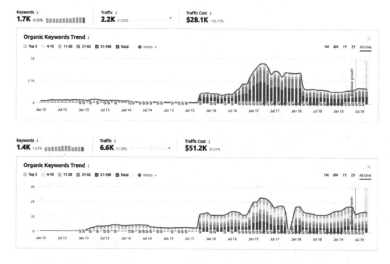

Notice how the corporate site ranks for more keywords (1.7k), but the traffic value is almost three times higher on the microsite.

Because the microsite ranks for keywords that are *so much* more valuable and in much better positions, it provides massive amounts of revenue to the company.

Wait, people always ask me, how does a separate site ranking help their business, though?

I always get that question after showing what microsites can accomplish. Without an understanding of tracking pixels, it's tough to grasp.

All of the pages of almost every site we touch have tracking pixels on them. This means that we can target people who have landed on pages with ads for whatever we'd like.

So, when someone is searching for "best _____ companies in the US," and they land on our microsite, they are immediately "tagged" by us. We can now show them ads for resources on the corporate site.

Or we could offer them resources in exchange for their contact information on the microsite.

Either way, we now have an audience of people who have searched for a phrase that clearly identifies them as a great potential customer.

A Branding Recommendation

I want to recommend that if you use this strategy, which is possibly one of the most valuable in this entire book, to brand the microsites properly. You don't want to be misleading with your microsite.

Our recommendation to customers is always to put a "powered by abc company" or "brought to you by xyz company" below the logo. You can get some pretty rough press if you appear to be misleading at all.

MAKING FRIENDS WITH PEOPLE WHO ALREADY HAVE YOUR AUDIENCE

Building a microsite can help you own the real estate, so to speak, that your potential customers are visiting. However, there are people right this moment who are already ranking for those searches. Many of them are likely not competitors.

We have seen many cases where sites will rank for a sought after phrase just because they created a resource years ago that got some attention.

Have your team do a ton of research into the most searched for keywords, create a list of the pages that already rank for those phrases, and reach out! Once you get them on the phone, ask them if you can place a tracking pixel on their site. Now, you want to be sure that they are letting people know on their site (typically through their privacy policy) that they are sharing visitor info with you.

You can also create resources for them that they will gladly exchange for mentions of your site.

Just be creative. Find out what they need help with and trade it for exposure to their audience who already needs your products and/or services. It's so easy to do a search for who they are, and most sites have a contact form or phone number.

It's important to note that laws are changing quickly around what has to be disclosed around privacy and tracking, so be sure to get legal advice on this before you do it. Every country is different. Even many states are different. I'm not an attorney and do not offer any legal advice.

SOMETHING WORKING IN PPC? DO IT AGAIN!

We are going to walk through affiliate marketing in great detail later, but it's important to quickly note that the strategy we're going over now is used by the most successful affiliate marketing campaigns.

The idea is based on the fact that there's only so much real estate available on the screen after doing a search in the search engines. With that in mind, if you increase the amount of real estate you control, the more successful you'll be.

We often create landing pages for clients and push people to them through paid search marketing. This is a strategy we've already outlined. However, to maximize results, you can create additional domains with similar landing pages and partner with people to run campaigns to those as well. This can be done by paying the people you partner with some kind of fee per lead generated, or some kind of fixed rate.

Most search engines aren't fond of the same person buying the same keywords under different accounts. But if there's a unique offering from a different company, and you have a relationship with that company, it's in line with all of the terms of service I'm familiar with.

Use your own judgement here, and don't be irresponsible. The moment you try to have your team do something shady, it will come back to haunt you and accounts will get shut down.

PAID CLICKS COME FROM MORE THAN JUST SEARCHES

I'm often surprised when I share some of the unique ways that Google Ads can be used to get messaging in front of potential clients.

Again and again, I'm shocked that almost no executives know what's possible. Many are angry their teams aren't doing it already. Before you blow a gasket though, understand that your team is not you. So, while you have a vision for the possibilities and can link a "tool" with a possibility, it's unfair to expect your team to make those same connections.

Let's go over some more advanced possibilities with Google Ads—things beyond having an ad come up when someone does a search.

RETARGETING & INTENT

Before we get into the places where you can put your message, understand that in all these cases, you have multiple approaches. You can base the ad being shown to people who have already been on a page of your site (retargeting pixels), or shown to anyone, regardless of whether they've visited your site before.

You can also exclude people who have been on certain pages of your site.

Let's say you have a page that only your active clients visit. You can tell Google *not* to show ads to those people, avoiding wasting money or the risk of potentially annoying loyal customers.

SPECIFIC VIDEOS ON YOUTUBE

By now you should know that YouTube is more than just videos of people jumping into water imitating a "silly salmon" or performing pranks on their friends.

It actually has an incredible number of helpful videos, and many of them are watched by people who want or need your products and services. To take this further, there are probably videos that would logically *only* be watched by people who are your potential customers.

For example, let's imagine you sell a car detailing product. After doing a quick search, I discovered a video ranking at the top of YouTube when people search for "car detailing products" (see below).

Notice that there have been 84,000 views of this video over two weeks. That's some pretty solid traffic.

It would be a logical statement to say that the people watching this video are interested in car detailing products, right? Using Google Ads, your team can create an ad that shows to people who watch this video specifically.

Types of Ads

At the time of writing, there are seven different types of YouTube ads. These include skippable TrueView ads, non-skippable pre-roll ads, bumper ads, display ads, overlay ads, sponsored cards, and masthead ads.

YouTube advertising changes constantly, so rather than get into details on each, I'll let you use Google to find the current ad types and the methods to get them rocking. The important thing to understand is that there are many different ways to get your message in front of people, including having your message come up when people are watching specific videos.

Specific Video Channels On YouTube

Here's a hypothetical scenario to kick around. Let's pretend your business helps people who are using Salesforce.com lower their phone costs.

You can target people who are watching videos on the Salesforce.com YouTube channel. Using the same ad types we just went over, you can make it so anyone who watches any video on specific YouTube channels sees your ad. Here is what the Salesforce.com YouTube Channel looks like currently:

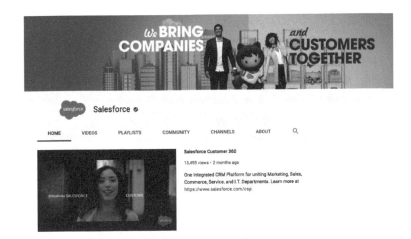

The possibilities with YouTube are endless. Take the time to learn about them and test to come up with different ways of getting your message out to the world effectively.

FUN FACT: Think about this as well. Have a competitor who has the same clients you want? Consider having ads for your product or service run on their videos and channels that have clear messaging related to how switching to you could save them time, money, and stress.

DISPLAY NETWORK

There are probably popular sites that help your potential customers with solutions to their challenges. Many of these sites allow display ads to run on them through Google Ads. You can create videos, animated, images, or text ads to run on these sites and specifically pick them within the Google Ads interface.

In addition, it's possible to target only people who are reading a page that contains very specific text. This can be done on specific sites, or in general around the web.

Display ads also power advertising within many apps. While we don't typically use this, it can be great for retargeting. Let's say someone is considering your product or service. Suddenly they start seeing your logo everywhere around the web. They even start seeing your logo within apps. Surely their confidence in you will build. Or, if the targeting is too heavy and frequent, it may build irritation. So be careful in walking this line around exposure and return.

ADS IN GMAIL

Did you know you can have ads   show up at the top of Gmail account user's inbox? We have found this to be a great strategy if someone is considering a proposal.

You can place a pixel within the page where they download the proposal and another on a page where only paid clients go.

Then you set it up in your Google Ads account to show Gmail ads to people who have been flagged by the proposal pixel but not the paid client pixel. Gear the ad message toward accepting the proposal and getting started. You'll only pay when someone actually opens the email.

THE MONEY'S IN THE SPLIT

At almost every CEO Leadership event I speak at, I say, "raise your hand if your business has ever tried paid traffic." Typically, about three-quarters of the room raises their hand.

"Great," I say, "keep your hand up if you *no longer* do paid traffic."

Almost every hand stays up.

"Okay," I go on. "Somebody tell me why you don't run it any longer, please."

"It didn't work," is the response almost every time. "We spent more than we made."

My typical answer: "I respect that. How many split tests did you have your team do?"

Blank stares. Can you see the problem?

THE COMPETENCE / EMPOWERMENT / PATIENCE CHALLENGE

There are three things every successful digital marketer needs. One, they have to be **competent** in their knowledge and strategy. Two, they need to feel **empowered** to spend money and test theories to find the strategies that do and don't work. And third, they have to have **patience** to wait for the results to come in after the testing has been done.

Successful digital marketing can be compared with panning for gold. You're constantly panning without great results. You get small wins here and there. But then something magical happens. You find a vein of gold and follow it. And suddenly you start raking in the gold.

Many paid search and social experts say 80 percent of the campaigns you launch won't work. But 20 percent will have a huge ROI. The problem is that most business executives don't **empower** their teams to do the proper testing and exploring. They either lack confidence in their team's **competence**, or don't have the **patience** to let them do what they need to have success. Don't be that kind of boss. Give your people the tools and time they need to succeed in an unpredictable field.

Split testing is at the core of almost every hugely successful campaign. Let's dig into a fictitious example.

Let's say you have a product that earns you a profit of $100 each sale. You pay $10 per click and you convert 1 out of 15 clicks into a sale. You're losing money.

You're spending $150 to profit $100. Your conversion rate in this case is about 6.7 percent. A great marketer will get excited about this though because it's proof that the campaign will create revenue.

In order to break even, though, we need to get to at least a 10 percent conversion rate.

Digging in, the marketer sees that clicks from iPhones are converting at 14 percent, but clicks from Samsung devices only convert at 4 percent. So the marketer pauses all traffic from people using phones other than iPhones. Now your conversion rate jumps up to 14 percent.

You're making money. You're converting 1.4 sales for every $100 spent. So every time you spend $100, you're profiting $140. #win.

This is a situation that isn't as far-fetched as you may think. The problem is that many executives aren't giving the time to competent people and allowing them to make mistakes before cutting the budget.

SOFTWARE FOR THE WIN

There are great software packages that are affordable that allow you to split test easily. We prefer VWO.com. We also use Hotjar for a lot of analysis.

These software packages are extremely affordable, will allow your team to create visual breakdowns of what's happening with your traffic, and will help achieve profitability.

With Hotjar, you can actually watch people as they visit the landing pages your team puts together. You can even see where those visitors are clicking and at what point in their visits. It also allows you to create heat maps and much more.

SPLIT TESTING EXAMPLES

Here are some examples of split testing that you may be able to quickly ask your team to implement. As you read through these, think of pages you already have on your site that could help you find more clients than they do today.

FORM LOCATION

One customer went completely against the grain and moved their form from the right side of the page to the middle of the page instead. Most designers would assume a change like this would be horrible for conversions.

Their results? Moving the form to the center of the page increased their conversion rate from 11% to 16%.– That's an almost 50% increase!

CAPITALIZATION OF HEADLINES, URLS, ETC.

There have been thousands of tests done that show ads in Google are clicked on more when capital letters are used in domain names. Now, Google doesn't allow this any longer, but what a great example for things like email copy, title tags, etc.

THE WORDING OF CALLS TO ACTION

Look at these examples:

A.   Get $10 off your purchase. Book online now!
B.   Get an additional $10 off. Book online now!

Which do you think would have the best conversion rate?

The winner was B. And the CTR (click through rate) **doubled**.

Without testing them, they would have lost out on a ton of revenue.

TESTING, TESTING, TESTING, OH MY!

There really is no end to the number of things you can split test. Head over to Google and search for "Things to split test landing page," and you'll find amazing resources.

GOING LOCO ... OR LOCAL I MEAN

If you have many locations or have a business that is extremely targeted to a particular community, it's important to make sure that Google Maps and other mapping platforms have the correct information.

When these aren't set up properly, it can negatively affect your search engine rankings, as well as apps and sites that focus on local reviews and information.

We actually created a tool at local.conklinmedia.com where you can check your status on many of these factors.

While I could write an entire book on local digital marketing, the main thing to be clear about is that Google is hyper focused on providing local solutions to people Google believes are in search of a local solution.

Here's an incredible guide you can pass along to your team that will help you get up to speed with Google My Business, which powers much of the local digital sphere.

https://blog.hubspot.com/marketing/google-my-business

ADVANCED PAID SEARCH & SOCIAL

There's a reason why there are employees in paid traffic positions earning $20,000 per year, and also employees in those same positions who make $100,000 plus per year.

The ones who earn more do so by using their brains. Any person capable of going on the internet and watching a 5-minute video can run a paid traffic campaign.

Simply upload some keywords, write some ads, and boom: done.

However, the people who actually make a ton of money for their clients are the ones who get paid incredibly well. And making a ton of money almost never happens without constant tests, digging into the depths of reporting, turning off and on specific demographics, audiences, keywords and their match types, testing ad scheduling, etc.

TARGETING IN GOOGLE, AND WHOEVER ELSE SHOWS UP

Pixels are simply invisible images that load on someone's device so they can be tracked later. We don't need to get into the details here, but if you need to understand more about the technology behind pixels, just Google "how Facebook pixels work," and you'll get a lot of resources.

Facebook pixels are important because they allow you to target people who have seen specific content on your site. If you sell products, for example, and someone landed on a page for "Product A" but never landed on the payment confirmation-page, you could target them with ads on either Instagram or Facebook for that specific product. It's also powerful enough so that anyone who ends up landing on the confirmation-page is then removed from seeing those ads.

Businesses that provide (or could provide) digital proposals can install Facebook or other pixels where those proposals are located. You could then share testimonial ads (advertisements that feature photos of customers, videos of customers, and even employees along with favorable quotes about your company) to the people who have seen the proposal but have not yet become customers.

This technology gives an incredible amount of power to support your marketing efforts.

"Oh, but my audience isn't on Facebook," you say, "and if they were, they don't make business buying decisions there." Many executives believe this, and they are *all* wrong.

We have seen an unbelievable amount of B2B companies benefit from Facebook Ads powered by pixels. Often times, they're targeting people who have come from a search engine looking for a very specific industrial product. That company is then all over the web, or so it seems to the individuals being targeted.

I'm not sure I've ever seen a campaign's conversion rates *not* go up after implementing retargeting through pixels.

AD SCHEDULING

It's possible to have ads run to certain people at specific times and at other times target different people or even stop running.

This is, once again, something that's commonly ignored because it either takes too much effort to test, people simply don't understand how to make it happen, or don't even know it's possible.

A client came to us once with a campaign that was failing. It was generating revenue, but the money being made was much less than what they were spending. There was no profit being made and they were throwing money down the drain.

They were looking at campaign costs versus income from the campaign at a macro level. But there was unseen gold once you got into the micro levels. This is a common situation, by the way.

This particular scenario involved ad scheduling.

We found that there was a lot of "looky-loo" junk traffic coming to the site from the campaign between the hours of 11 p.m. and 7 a.m. We could tell because the bounce rates in Google Analytics were almost double with traffic from the source in question at that time.

We were able to make the campaign profitable by simply turning the ads off during those hours.

Be sure not to make the mistake of assuming overnight traffic is always lower converting, though. We have actually noticed internally that a lot of advertisers paying for the same keywords as us turn their ads off at night. This puts our ads at a higher position due to decreased competition.

GEOGRAPHY

This one is huge. It's possible to advertise in specific areas, and you can get extremely specific.

When I started using Google search ads in the early 2000's you "could", in theory, market by geography, but it was really poor. The tech keeps getting better and better.

If you look at your reporting and analytics on a macro level and segment by cities, you'll often find some crazy data. For example, maybe a specific city has a few advertisers that are aggressive and you're just not converting in that area. You could make the choice to either pause the campaigns, or increase your budget to get more leads in only those specific geographies.

DEMOGRAPHICS

Similar to the above, you can show ads to people who meet certain demographic requirements.

I like to start by showing ads to everyone, unless it's a *very* specific audience I'm interrupting. Consider feminine hygiene, for example, you'd only show ads to women likely, and potentially women in certain age groups.

However, it's certainly possible that dads may click on ads for their daughters or search for solutions in homes where there's no female to assist.

Always use big data to make the micro decisions. By doing so you can expect to move into profitability as you continue to make micro adjustments to your campaigns.

TRACKING EVERYTHING SO YOU KNOW THE ROI

My most passionate moments in my career come when I'm in a room with an executive sharing all the results we have achieved for them. The reason I'm able to do that and definitively show that it's coming from our efforts (or the efforts of others), is because we take the time to set up tracking properly.

Setting up tracking is a very technical task, and this book is not intended to teach the intricate technical details.

Instead of explaining the "how," I'm going to go over the "what" and the "why."

GOOGLE ANALYTICS

If you have seen the benefits of analytics in terms of understanding your business, how customers respond to you and interact with your site, this next sentence may shock you. About 30 percent of the executives I speak with *still* don't have Google Analytics installed on their site. Many who do, don't have goal tracking or demographic tracking turned on. This blows my mind, but those statistics are a part of why I felt this specific book needed to be written.

Google Analytics is what provides the X-ray for you and your team to help make decisions about what to do next. If you're still using "hits" as a descriptor when talking about your website's traffic, you need to come to terms with the fact that you're still living in the late 90's.

Installing Google Analytics is one of the simplest tasks possible with today's content management systems.

Your team simply has to paste the following text (with your unique Google Analytics provided code, of course) into either the CMS header or footer file.

```
<!-- Google Analytics -->
<script>
(function(i,s,o,g,r,a,m){i['GoogleAnalyticsObject']=r;i[r]=i[r]||function(){
(i[r].q=i[r].q||[]).push(arguments)},i[r].l=1*new Date();a=s.createElement(o),
m=s.getElementsByTagName(o)[0];a.async=1;a.src=g;m.parentNode.insertBefore(a,m)
})(window,document,'script','https://www.google-analytics.com/analytics.js','ga');

ga('create', 'UA-XXXXX-Y', 'auto');
ga('send', 'pageview');
</script>
<!-- End Google Analytics -->
```

GOAL TRACKING

Once you have tracking installed, you empower your team to do things like goal tracking. I'll share a story in a later chapter about how a company made an additional $1.7 million in revenue because of a split testing discovery. This discovery was possible because goal tracking was set up.

The things you can track, especially when you have actions (called events) in place using Google Tag Manager along with Google Analytics, are nearly endless. How much time do people on specific types of computers or in specific cities spend on a page? Do men or women scroll deeper on a specific page's content? Do the people who come to our page from Facebook make us enough money to cover our social media ad spend? All of these questions, and thousands more, can be answered with goal tracking installed.

DEMOGRAPHICS TRACKING

There is a simple toggle button (followed by a confirmation window) to turn on demographic tracking. Doing so let's you go even more in depth.

Affinity categories, which allow you to understand what other types of sites your visitors are going to, is one of the most powerful things you can see in demographic tracking.

This can be incredible information to have when you're working on offline campaigns and more.

GOOGLE TAG MANAGER

Google Analytics is the main thing that *must* be done on every single website without fail, unless you have an alternative tracking source, like Clicky or another software.

However, Tag Manager can be seen as more of a priority to many because it's basically a "box" that holds all of the remaining things we're going to talk about, in addition to Analytics. The only reason I mention it second is because Google Analytics is definitely the priority.

In addition, when you install Google Tag Manager, it allows you to enable certain settings that make tracking events on your site possible.

Call Tracking

I started using call tracking with Ifbyphone.com (now DialogTech), years ago, well before it was even popular in digital marketing circles. I found myself getting frustrated when the work I was doing for clients resulted in people visiting their website and then calling. These calls would often be a catalyst for new customers, and the digital marketing campaigns didn't get credit for it. Today, DialogTech is offering even more advanced services and features to help solve that problem.

You need to know when an email you send results in a phone call and how much that customer ended up spending in order to make the most effective decisions with your digital marketing efforts.

Setting up call tracking is as simple as adding a code to your site. This can often be done through Google Tag Manager.

After you set it up, you can track first time calls as well as repeat calls. This becomes incredibly beneficial because people will often just redial a previously dialed number. You don't want those leads to count more than once.

Calls can be traced back to specific sources as well as specific keywords or ads. They are then logged as leads so you can see which keywords or ads are the ones generating the calls. Check out DialogTech.com or CallRail.com for more info.

At this moment in time, in our current digital business climate, I would *never, ever* do a campaign without call tracking.

If your team is going to dig into call tracking, make sure you have them research integrating it with Google Analytics, allowing you to combine call data with your other data.

Hotjar (Or Other Screen Tracking)

When you launch a new campaign, it's imperative to understand how people are interacting with the content you're sending them to. Hotjar and other screen tracking analytics programs allow you to watch videos of people on your site. You can see mouse movements, scrolling, etc. Many people on computers read with their mouse, so you can almost always see what they're reading and where they are looking.

Extremely powerful data can be discovered when you make changes to a page and then watch the videos to see how people react differently.

It's obviously difficult to watch everything, so these platforms also allow you to create heat maps that show collected data in one image with blue to red indicators.

AFFILIATE MARKETING: HIRE HUNDREDS OF COMMISSION ONLY SALES PEOPLE ALL AT ONCE

When asked if they would be excited to bring on qualified commission-only sales people to help grow their business, 95 percent of business owners emphatically say "yes!" Yet, when you ask them if they have empowered their teams to take on affiliate marketing, those same blank stares come again.

I have no idea why so few business leaders use affiliate marketing as a growth strategy. Again, I *believe* it's mostly due to the lack of understanding we've talked about in these pages.

HOW AFFILIATE MARKETING WORKS

It's pretty simple, really. There are three "players" involved:

YOUR BUSINESS <-> AFFILIATE NETWORK <-> AFFILIATES

First, your business contacts an affiliate network and offers some kind of a commission on sales or leads of your products/services to the affiliate network.

The affiliate network then gives your information to affiliates and offers the affiliates a portion of what you're paying them per sale/lead of your products/services.

Finally, the affiliates begin to market your products/services to their audiences via landing pages, search campaigns, social campaigns, email campaigns, etc.

The technicalities of how it all works can basically be summed up by understanding tracking codes. The affiliate network you work with will assign unique tracking codes to its affiliates. When the affiliates link to your site using these unique tracking codes, the affiliate network is able to discover which affiliates are sending the traffic, as well as any sales/lead data associated with it.

There are generally expiration dates as well, which you can work with your affiliate network to set. If, for example, you'd like to give credit for a max of 30 days to an affiliate, you can do that. In other words, if someone follows an affiliate link to your site and makes a decision that does not result in a sale, but comes back 20 days late, they would still be credited for that sale. If they came back after the 30 day expiration, however, they would not be credited for that sale.

Some companies give affiliates the run of their entire site, meaning that anything a person buys gets credited to the affiliate. Other times, the company will choose to provide a commission on only one or a few products or services.

Everything is negotiable, but the single most important thing to consider is the affiliate network, and who's going to manage the campaign for you. You can have the best affiliate program offerings in the world, but you really need super affiliates to make it go. I recommend working closely with your affiliate network to make that happen.

SOME AFFILIATE NETWORKS TO CONSIDER

There are hundreds of affiliate networks. It's important that you find one that has affiliates who have experience working with companies or offers similar to yours.

I'll provide you with a few of the affiliate networks I personally have experience with, but they change constantly, so by the time you're reading this, it's likely that they have been bought, sold, changed names, etc. So simply go to your favorite search engine and type in "top affiliate networks" and you'll learn a lot.

COMMISSIONJUNCTION (CJ)
HTTPS://CJ.COM

CJ has some of the biggest brands on the planet as advertisers, and therefore has many successful affiliates. The company was founded in 1998. It's now part of Publicis Media Groupe, a publicly traded company in France.

Some of the world's largest brands use CJ as their affiliate network of choice, including:

- GoPro
- Lowe's
- Office Depot

And they have some huge publishers as well:

- CNN
- TIME
- Wirecutter

SHAREASALE
HTTPS://SHAREASALE.COM

ShareASale is known to have good payout schedules, a large network, and great affiliates. In fact, ShareASale has more than 4,000 advertisers. About 1,000 of them have made exclusive agreements with them guaranteeing that they won't use any other networks outside of ShareASale.

MAXBOUNTY
HTTPS://MAXBOUNTY.COM

I love MaxBounty for their lead-generation campaigns. For people reading this book who have B2B businesses or service based businesses, this is a great affiliate network to talk to.

They are becoming increasingly focused on quality, and are taking massive measures to end spam challenges that are present in the industry today.

CREATE NEW STREAMS OF REVENUE AS AN AFFILIATE AS WELL!

Affiliate marketing also makes it easy to earn additional revenue from your existing customers, in addition to generating new sales and revenue.

For example, we have a client who is in the automotive space, and they were able to add $50,000+ per year in gross revenue through an affiliate partnership with an auto warranty company.

This can be done by adding an additional purchasing option in the checkout, sending emails to clients, or (my favorite) making money from clients who weren't previously the "right" type of customers for you.

Your team can create a free account. Then you can easily see a list of companies you can partner with through your affiliate network account in order to create new revenue.

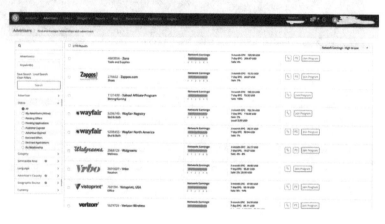

THE TEAM YOU NEED & WHAT YOU SHOULD OUTSOURCE

This is actually one of my favorite topics. I didn't really cover it at my speaking events until I started getting asked the question more frequently. I would talk with CEOs about how to use digital communication to grow their companies, and they, for the most part understood what needed to be done. However, they really didn't get all of the different talents and positions that are out there and how to actually find them.

A GEEK IS NOT JUST A GEEK

Depending on how old you are, you may remember when family doctors handled mostly everything. Whether your ear hurts or your foot hurts, you'd go to "the doctor."

Today, however, we've got doctors who specialize in just about every area of the body. Some of these doctors not only focus on a specific area, but they focus on a specific condition of that area. While they are focused on these areas, they also have a general understanding of the rest of the body and how their area of focus relates and interacts with it.

Digital communication professionals work in the exact same way. Some of the common areas of focus include web programming, web design, paid social media, paid search, organic search (SEO), data analysis, copywriting, graphic design, marketing automation, email marketing, and much more.

Business leaders are often shocked when I share with them that in our industry it's not reasonable to expect a web designer to design high-end business cards. We also can't expect that web designer to write the copy for the site they're designing. The web designer understands how their designs interact and work with copy and the importance of brand consistency with business cards, but the skill set of a web designer is focused on things like CSS, HTML, and (maybe) a little bit of PHP, but definitely not content writing.

Another common mistake is when well-intentioned business leaders put a web designer in charge of a site redesign without having an SEO specialist involved (oh, by the way, there are on-page and off-page SEO specialists, and in this case we need an on-page SEO specialist). When the new site launches, the traffic plummets. Therefore the leads and calls plummet too. The CEO doesn't even notice it, because he or she is Lost @ 30,000 Feet. But then the marketing VP gets upset with the website designer, and the sales VP says the marketer is doing a bad job because leads are down.

Seriously, this **exact** story has played out at least 250 times in my 20 year career.

The problem is that the web designer doesn't even know that an SEO specialist should be involved because they don't know what they don't know.

THE TALENTS

Our team is made up of people who cover the following talents:

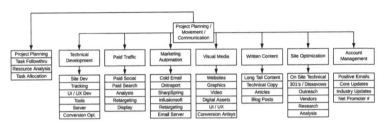

We're going to go through these, one by one. My recommendation would be to grab a pen and jot down what areas you have and haven't covered in your business. We often rank each talent 1-10 to give us an idea of how solid we are in that area. It can give you an idea of where you're weakest, and may need to "upgrade" talent, whether it's on your internal team or outsourced.

A quick note: we also like people to feel that they are able to grow in compensation and title. Therefore, we will give people titles that grow with experience. For us, the "ladder" includes the following terms tacked on to their job description:

- Coordinator or Assistant
- Associate
- Strategist
- Manager
- Director
- Officer

A web designer will often start as a Web Design Associate because we don't hire many entry-level people with that talent. In most cases, people out of college would start as an assistant or coordinator and move their way up with experience.

We also like to give specific measurable goals for our team members to hit that will put them at the next level. These often include achieving client goals or company goals in areas that they are specifically responsible.

Project Planning / Movement / Communication

Because marketing is done by so many people with so many unique talents in today's business climate, it's imperative to have an individual who is coordinating the movement of your marketing campaigns as well as making sure that all of the individuals on the same team are in sync.

For example, let's say you're building a search marketing campaign that's offering a free in-home consultation. Then, at that in-home consultation the salesperson gives *some* of the prospects they can't close a 25% off discount, but not the ones they close. You would probably want your marketing automation and retargeting teams to be showing retargeted reminders to the people who were offered that coupon specific ad so they have it at the top of their mind. The only way to do this is to have a specific page that the prospect who is offered the discount visit that the other prospects do not.

Can you imagine coordinating all of that without one person steering the ship? It would be nearly impossible. At least, I wouldn't be able to do it.

Now this role can certainly be played by a Chief Marketing Officer or Marketing VP, but they are often thinking at a much higher level about brand initiatives and such.

This individual also needs to have a clear understanding of how all of the marketing channels and talents work. They don't need to know how to code, but they do need to have a general understanding of how coders operate and how code operates, as well as a general understanding of different programming languages. To have the respect of the team, they need to have experience and know what's going on.

Project Planning

The first aspect of this role is planning out projects. This starts with understanding what the goals of the company are. Too often, we see Lost @ 30,000 Feet executives not sharing the actual business drivers with their marketing team.

Your marketing team needs to understand your business goals and challenges if you want them to be empowered and capable of helping you fix them.

Once they have specific business goals to achieve, the brainstorming meeting will take place. This meeting is a free-for-all that everyone in the marketing and sales teams should attend and offer input in. You'll find that some of your quietest team members are actually rock stars when given the opportunity.

Every idea is written down. We use a tool called MindMup where we just dump stuff. It basically creates an organized "map" of the brainstorming session.

Then the leaders within the marketing and sales teams (make sure all talents are covered) meet and organize the brainstorming map into an organized chart. You can use our ProfitPaths® Planning Sheets for this.

We also use LucidChart to create maps that breakdown how everything talks to everything–what happens when potential customers do specific things, land on specific pages, etc.

By having the leaders of all the teams doing the work involved together (this includes outsourcers), you'll have great input. More importantly, you'll have buy-in from all of those who participated in the final plan. Lastly, they will understand what they're supposed to do much more clearly.

Task Allocation

Now that the final "picture" of what success looks like is completed, a task list and some deadlines need to be put together.

We use a tool called Asana for this at our company. We don't recommend tasking the entire thing out, because it's common for things to change as people have better ideas or algorithms shift. Instead, have everyone agree to specific things to be done in the next week, and then schedule a meeting for everyone to come back together so they can each present what they accomplished to the group.

Task Follow Through

When the weekly measurable tasks are allocated to the team, a great project manager will ask each team member to schedule time on his or her calendar to accomplish the task.

Afterward, a quick follow up and check ins should be done with each team member every day. This can be done during a stand-up meeting in the morning with everyone, or through quick one-on-ones using a tool like Slack.

This isn't only being done to ensure that everyone is on task, it's being done to keep everyone in sync. The Project Manager is the one person who truly understands every aspect of a project in and out. Everyone else is isolated to their own challenges. In these complex marketing projects, each person's work, challenges, and limitations affect everyone else. With daily check-ins, the Project Manager can help each person by knowing what every other person is dealing with.

At the weekly meetings, each team member should literally *demonstrate* to the team what they did. This is important because it's easy for someone to "fake it." It's not that we distrust or look down on anyone, but it's so important to catch challenges early that could potentially change the way the project turns out or progresses.

Resource Analysis

It's also the responsibility of the Project Manager to analyze and plan human resource and talent needs. By knowing how much time is going to be needed by a specific "talent" to accomplish the goals of the projects, a Project Manager can inform your HR and finance teams of upcoming hiring needs.

In addition, there may be tools utilized by the team that are heading toward maximum usage capacity. Because this individual is responsible and understands the entire scope of projects, it's their responsibility to make recommendations to your leadership team in these areas.

MARKETING AUTOMATION

This is the only other position that needs to have a full understanding of the entire project from start to finish. The Marketing Automation Specialist is responsible for creating the communication that takes place between your brand and the potential customer, employee, etc.

The individual in this role needs to have a deep understanding of cold email outreach, relational email strategies, transactional email best practices, retargeting strategies & platforms, and a broad understanding and ability to learn quickly different marketing automation platforms.

Cold Email

Cold email is one of the single most effective and profitable strategies available today. It's especially effective in B2B campaigns. There are some amazing companies, like DiscoverOrg.com who provide incredibly reliable and accurate data that includes email addresses of professionals. They are also extremely expensive ($25,000+ per year and require a contract). Once you have a list and can create a truly valuable resource or tool the people you're emailing would appreciate, you can send them emails to tell them about it.

Your content team will write the emails, your visual team will design the landing pages, and your Marketing Automation Specialist will send and automate the process.

It will also be important for this individual to ensure that the individuals being emailed are included in the database of the marketing automation software you're using so everyone can be properly tracked.

Relational Email

Once relationships have been established, the Marketing Automation Specialist is responsible to keep the communication lines open with those potential customers through retargeting (see below) and relational email. These emails will be sent out from the marketing automation software and are often time released and based on specific pages that the potential customer has visited.

Transactional Email

Transactional emails are between your brand and current customers. They can include billing emails, newsletter updates, product updates, or emails sent with the goal of getting referrals.

These are sometimes sent within the marketing automation software but could be built into a CRM or other internal system. Either way, they are the responsibility of the Marketing Automation Specialist.

Retargeting

The ads that potential customers see as you take them through your ProfitPath®, use Google Ads, Facebook Ads, and the other platforms we've talked about, like AdRoll. All of these platforms need to have oversight by the same person who is managing the marketing automation software so that the messaging stays consistent across the board.

Once again, the ads are designed by the visual team, coordinated by the Project Manager, but the marketing automation specialist coordinates with the paid traffic specialist to get them in front of the right people.

Marketing Automation Software

There are many platforms and the right one for your goals may be different than someone else's. We've used many of them, including Ontraport, Infusionsoft (now Keap), Pardot (works with Salesforce.com), SharpSpring, HubSpot, and others.

Your Marketing Automation Specialist needs to be familiar with these platforms as well as new ones that hit the market. He or she is also responsible for running the software platform you choose and helping the team when there are weak areas or areas that need to be optimized.

Email Server / List Cleansing / Opt Outs

Email is a huge part of this role, as mentioned above. Therefore, it's important for this component's keepers to work with the Technical

Development team to make sure your email server is healthy, your list is clean, and to keep on top of opt outs from your campaigns.

Each separate email in violation of the CAN-SPAM Act is subject to penalties of up to $42,530, so non-compliance can be costly. Read more here: https://www.ftc.gov/tips-advice/business-center/guidance/can-spam-act-compliance-guide-business

VISUAL MEDIA (DESIGN)

This team is in charge of everything and anything that your campaign audience actually sees. It's important to understand that you shouldn't expect to find all of these talents we're going through in one individual. Most of them are completely separate tasks. We've learned that if you're willing to shell out more cash, you can find rare people who have a combination of these skills.

The Visual Media team isn't responsible for the writing within a campaign. Writers and designers almost always work closely together to accomplish the goals of these campaigns.

There is an ongoing friendly (sometimes) chicken and egg debate between writing professionals and designers in the marketing industry as to which comes first: writing or design. Personally, I'm of the belief that the design should be created with what we call "lorem ipsum" (fake text). (Note: My Visual Media Director, Adam, didn't actually want me to include this in the book. I respect his opinion a lot and want to make sure his thoughts are here as well). The writer is then responsible for filling in text for the design. However, there are people who are much more talented in these departments than I am who would disagree and say the design should be made after the writing has been done.

Website Design

Today, almost all sites are designed using some type of CMS (content management system). These include WordPress, Shopify, Drupal, and the Myspace builder (that's a joke).

Platform Experience

To effectively web design today, a web designer needs to have extensive experience with these platforms. As of 2019, WordPress is the undisputed champ for website building, even large corporate sites.

There are times where something more complicated will be needed, but 90 percent of the time a custom WordPress buildout will work just fine.

CSS Knowledge

CSS is a language that changes how text, images, and more are displayed in a user's browser. A website designer will have advanced knowledge of this language.

Design Best Practices

It's really important for your website designer to understand things like image optimization, CRO (conversion rate optimization), and much more. Additionally, I've seen many designers lose their "touch" with new visual styles, development standards, and software to create better efficiency. It's important that when you're looking for that perfect individual to help with your visual design you ask about how they plan to handle the changes in their field over time.

Graphics

Graphics include things like white papers, brochures, business cards, logos, and other visual content. Even the interface that users work with to manipulate tools your tech team may develop like calculators and assessments are included.

It's important to note that many web designers are not great graphic designers. Laying out a site in a way that maximizes user experience is a completely different skill set than manipulating graphics. Many CEOs put those skill sets in the same category and make incorrect assumptions. Remember that the "found" at 30,000 Feet CEO, versus the one who is still "lost," understands that the marketing industry has gone the way of the health industry, where there are specialists for just about every type of challenge.

VIDEO

I'm a huge believer in video, which is quickly becoming the single most important type of content on the web. But there are many, many different talents and subsets to make it all happen. Let's unpack some of them.

Professional Video Production

Professional video can be used to create promotional content, but it's not really needed any longer to create things like webinars, how-to guides, educational content, or most types of video.

If you're going to be creating promotional content (think a speaker promotional video or Super Bowl commercial), it's important to understand that three different skill sets are often used. *Many* great videographers aren't great storytellers. Editors tend to be the storytellers. However, many storytellers aren't editors or shooters. They're often directors. And if you're hoping to bring any of those on staff full time, be prepared to pay significant salaries, because many of them are freelancers or own their own studios and can earn significantly more from their independent work than they can in an environment where they are compensated with a salary.

Animation

There are also animators who can truly bring content to life through moving illustrations and other forms of animation. This is an additional skill that won't be found in 99 percent of people who match the video talent types described above.

If you go to Upwork, or even just Google, and search for "explainer video creator," you'll learn that there are literally thousands of people offering animation-type services. There are also software packages that can be purchased where you can develop less professional animated videos yourself. I personally don't recommend these lower-cost solutions—but they are there. Sometimes, you can use them as a leader in your organization to create a "demo" for a pro to look at so they can understand better what you're looking to accomplish, and then take it to the next level.

Webinars

Webinars aren't actually created by the visual team. Typically, you'll need to tap your sales team to get someone to run the webinar. However, we have had a lot of satisfaction in having our visual team look at our slide decks we create in PowerPoint and making them really pop for our webinars. I recommend this.

A quick note on webinars, which we'll cover in more depth later: We have found Zoom.us and WebinarJam as being some of the best solutions for webinars. If you're looking to have your webinars run constantly as a "sales force" of sorts, then EverWebinar is our current go to.

With EverWebinar, you can have a webinar that literally runs on a constant schedule but allows your attendees to interact like it's live.

Live Videos & Screencasts

Live videos and screencasts are becoming *huge* for meetings, educational content, and product demos. We use a software tool called ScreenFlow to create screencasts when we want to have a video that shows us, plus our screen. You can also configure these to create live videos on all the platforms. We aren't going to go into depth on the specific platforms that exist to do live video because they are changing so rapidly.

Digital Assets

Digital assets are guides, white papers, checklists, and other resources that are downloaded by someone, typically in exchange for an email so you can build out your email list.

We often use them as a way to introduce a company to strangers and give them a solid trust that our clients know what they're talking about. Once the asset is downloaded, we will often have them flow into a specific email campaign and show them specific ads in order to get them to the next stage in the journey of getting to know you and your brand.

The person that creates these digital assets is unique because they need to know how to use page layout software like InDesign or Illustrator. Many CEOs assume that if someone is a graphic designer, that they are good at page layout. Generally, this is far from the truth, unless you're spending a very high amount on a salary.

This individual should also understand how to optimize the file size of the PDF and if you really want a rockstar, they will also know how to make these resources animated and interactive online.

My advice is to outsource a lot of work like this after you have it created in an outline (even some content and a hand drawing) and find someone who has designed resources you love and has the elements you're looking for.

UX (User Experience) Design

A designer focused on UX is a researcher, copywriter, and often a tester. Their job is to determine how all of the different pieces of the puzzle, when brought together, are received and understood by the end user.

Some designers specialize in working directly with coders to create interfaces for things like apps, calculators, tools, etc. Many of these designers also have a slight understanding of how the code works and can make small modifications without involving a coder. In my business, I wouldn't hire a UX designer who couldn't do at least basic programming.

Any UX expert also understands the psychology behind the design. They should have a scientific reason why they do just about everything. This includes where a form is located on a page, specific words used in tool tips, and even button colors and how they change when hovered on.

UI (User Interface) Design

UI design is a subset of UX, but a vital one to make sure you have on your team if you're going to be building tool, applications, etc. The person focused on UI has the same goal of providing a great experience for the user, but this individuals focus is zeroed in on the actual buttons, links, graphics, language, etc. that are used by a user to interact with the product.

Conversion Analysis

On your tech team, you should have someone that can set up many different types of tracking that enable you to do split testing of content, landing pages, images, button colors, and more.

It's the design team's responsibility to create new things to be tested, all the time, based on the past results achieved. Within conversion optimization, you're looking to always be making incremental changes that increase conversion by small percentages.

We worked with a company in Dallas, Texas to increase a specific conversion in their process by 9 percent a year prior to this writing. This change/split test drove a $1.7 million increase in gross revenue. Small changes can be huge, but you need someone who understands what to test *and* has been given the authority from you to do so.

WRITTEN CONTENT

Next to video, there is nothing more important than written content. Every social platform, search platform, and tool uses the text that surrounds (and is within the code of) images, videos, and more to determine what it's about. Website pages are analyzed by search engines to learn what long tail phrases they should rank for (along with other factors included within SEO). There are a few types of content that writers need to be familiar with in order to create content for business growth campaigns.

Long Tail Content

Long tail content is so important that we've invested tens of thousands of dollars to create software that helps writers write it. Years ago, I did a search for "500 million dollar companies in Lancaster, PA," and discovered by complete mistake, the importance of long tail content as well as how to create it. The exact same strategies that worked then still work today.

Google shares a statistic that around 70 percent of keyword phrase searches have never been seen before by Google. However, when you analyze "silos" of keywords, as we talked about in earlier chapters, you discover that there are thousands and thousands of phrases for a head term. Logically, most of the phrases that are entered into Google that haven't been searched before include a mix of the unique words found within the phrases in the silo. Google and the other search engines use the content on your page to determine if your page should be listed in Google for these long tail search phrases.

If this is the case, you need to make sure you have as many of the words found within the silo phrases as you possibly can. Therefore, we use the lists of long tail phrases for the head term we want to rank for and create lists of the unique words found in them. We then make sure that each of these words is used in the content.

In my example above, "500 million dollar companies in Lancaster, PA," our website used to come up as the number 1 listing on Google. This was because on my page I had the following sentence:

"... is an Inc **500 Company**. We grew to more than $4.6 **million dollars** in 2007. We are located in **Lancaster, Pennsylvania**."

Because those words were included in the content, and there weren't any pages that were specifically about that rare search, Google put our site at the top. This was a huge light bulb for us and it completely changed the way that we saw on-site search optimization.

There are many keyword tools including Google Keyword Planner, SEMRush, Ahrefs, and more. Simply do a search for "best SEO keyword tools" and you'll find list upon list upon list.

Please understand, this skill set is not something that *any* writer I have ever met already knew how to do. It's something that is trained. Get in contact with us at LostAt30k.com and we have some content training there your writers can go through.

Every single piece of content you create that you want to rank in the search engines should go through this process. This includes blogs, articles, how-to guides, and (as I just stated) every single piece of content created.

Technical Content

Writers need to be able to get in the head of your company to create technical content. There are many people who are looking for help using products and services that are available through your company or your competitors. It's a very unique skill set to be able to write content that's technical, still written in layman's terms, and actually has a bit of entertainment value. However, those who do it will be rewarded.

The important thing to understand here is that if you have a significant amount of technical content, you can't expect your creative writing team to be happy writing it. This is something that is often best outsourced using tools like Upwork or even hitting up the engineering or science types in your organization.

Articles

There are a few reasons to have article writers in your company. Most of it is to support the SEO efforts we described. When someone on the SEO team gets an online site, newspaper, or community to publish content from your company, they are going to need a piece published. Also, there are times when a helpful article should be published on your site for a multitude of reasons. This is another time when an article writer will be asked to create content.

Blog Posts (and other editorial content)

Almost every company I encounter has completely misused blog posts since its inception. I have found that it's simply a lack of direction from the top in almost all of those cases.

The primary reason to have a blog is building confidence in your brand for those making a decision to work with you, whether they are considering a partnership or being a customer or working for you as an employee.

The second reason is blogs provide a place for the "linkerati" (Thanks, Rand) to reference on their sites.

The blog is not for things that aren't helpful, newsworthy, or emotional. People within the walls of a company have a very different perspective on what's of "interest," I think. Unfortunately, no one in the outside world really cares about half of the stuff I read on corporate blogs. If you want to see this for yourself Google "company blog," and go to page 4 of Google (this way you miss the .01 percent that's actually getting linked to because it's half interesting).

Blogs have two audiences: those who may link to the content (which is almost never your customers) and those who are looking to see if your company is worth their time and money. Create for those audiences, and create well. Nobody likes a lazy blogger.

SITE OPTIMIZATION

This is one of my favorite positions to talk about. I love site optimization, and it can be so powerful when administered by someone who knows what they're doing.

On-Site Technical SEO

Content For The Long Tail

The first step of on-site technical SEO is understanding what we talked about at the beginning of the book, search intent. After there are proven keywords we know are going to do well from our paid search efforts, we then begin to create content for those phrases. In the written content section we discussed how the writer writes long tail content. Getting this long tail content created is the first step.

Alt Tags, Heading Tags, Filenames, and URLs

Once that content is created, we need to make sure that the most popular words found within the list of phrases we pulled from are included within the alt tags of images, the file names included in the page, the URL, the H tags (especially the H1 tag), and within the links. I referenced the "Perfectly Optimized Page" content that Rand Fishkin did years ago as a resource here. That is *still* the page our team uses to make sure that our content is optimized properly.

Canonical Tags

Sometimes, there are multiple pages that have almost all of the same content on them. When this happens (e-commerce sites are common), it's important to have what's called a canonical tag. This lets the search engines know that you realize there are multiple pages that contain super similar content, but that you want it what way. It then "points" in the code to the page that you want to give the "credit" for.

Page Speed

Page speed became a huge factor for the search engines a few years ago. Google simply doesn't want to give its users a poor experience by recommending sites to its users that are slow. There are many ways to optimize for speed, and your Technical SEO pro needs to understand how to do so.

Mobile (AMP)

Google gives an opportunity to site owners to create "AMP" versions of pages that are heavily optimized for mobile devices.

When someone is using Google Mobile, these AMP pages load almost instantly when a Google user clicks on them. In Google's eyes (and I'm 100 percent sure this is backed up with data) this increased satisfaction.

Bounce Rate Optimization

It's been proven again and again in tests that the bounce rate of a page is a leading factor in Google's algorithm. The bounce rate is the percentage of people that hit a page and then click back. It's assumed that they didn't get what they wanted on the site.

This is another indicator of a poor web page to Google. Our team has done tests where we send social traffic to a page we knew followed best practices and would have a low bounce rate. The rankings on these pages would improve.

Make sure this is thought about and optimized by your team.

301 Redirects

Don't skip this. I find this is a **huge** issue at every speaking event I do. You know by now how important it is to have other web pages include links on them that take users to your site when they are clicked. These links point to specific pages of your site.

Often, if you have a project that's been completed, a product that no longer exists, or an event that is over, the page is removed from your site. What happens if you have a bunch of links pointing to those pages? They do something called 404. This tells whoever is looking at the page that it no longer exists.

Next question: would Google want to recommend a page to its users that doesn't exist any longer? No, it wouldn't because it doesn't create a positive experience.

Google also doesn't count any of the links that are pointing to your site when this happens! So all the links you've built in the past are now completely wasted. Don't get too excited. There's a solution, and it's easy. But let me share one extremely common time when this happens.

You or your team hire a fancy web design company to create a new look and feel for your company's web presence. Everyone is excited.

Then it launches.

Then the traffic *plummets.*

This happens so *often*! The reason is that the web design company changed the URLs of the pages. For example, maybe your "about" page was located at website.com/about_us and now it's located at website.com/aboutus. That one simple underscore missing just made every single link that points to /about_us not count any more to Google.

This lowers your authority in Google's eyes and will lower your ranking and therefore your traffic.

We had something similar to this happen with a real estate company. This particular company sold extremely expensive homes. When homes were listed by them first, they would almost always end up listed on the New York Times website. But when the listings sold and were no longer on the market, the real estate company removed the pages from its site. This created a broken link every single time and killed its rankings.

So, what's the solution? 301 redirects. You simply have your SEO team or tech team add a 301 redirect to the site that tells Google and web browsers to shift to a new webpage when the old one is entered.

With the real estate example, we had the old pages 301 redirect to a community page for other similar houses in the same area. For the record, they had an 80 percent increase in traffic over the next three months.

Duplicate Content

Duplicate content is a big problem for many sites. This happens for many reasons, including companies using copy and paste descriptions of products across multiple pages.

One solution is to make sure that your team places a "no index" tag on the pages that they don't wish to appear in the search engines.

Another is to use a canonical tag if you need the page to still appear for usability purposes and need the links that may come to the page to send credit elsewhere.

Outreach

Outreach is the most important task to have your team consistently do to help your search marketing. This can sometimes be more easily viewed as digital PR.

Here's the kicker. While it's the most important thing, it's also the thing I find being done the *least*. Most of the time it's the CEO's fault and a mistake made due to lack of understanding.

Outreach is when someone on your team, or a vendor, researches, and contacts sites that are authoritative in Google's eyes and relevant to what you do.

Once the owner or a writer for the site is connected with, the job turns into a sales role. Your team member needs to negotiate a way to get a link from that site to yours. This can be done by providing them with content that your site is referenced in, or by having something on your site that's so great, they are willing to link to it.

Most of the people who have become really skilled at this make a significant salary with an agency of some type, so be ready to pony up. You can usually compensate these individuals with a salary plus commission on links they get.

There are really four subsets to this position; site research, contact information research, outreach, and writing. Unless you want an incredibly high turnover on your team, don't expect the same individual to handle all of these tasks themselves. Here is how we break it all down.

We will often use virtual assistants to do the research, which is finding sites that are authoritative with some type of relevance to you. We are looking for sites that rank for a large number of keywords in Google.

We use this metric because it clearly shows the website is authoritative (to Google).

Collecting contact information is next and this is a job for an innovator. Someone who can be creative and use tools like Snov.io combined with LinkedIn, and be able to dig and dig efficiently and effectively.

The outreach can be initiated by a VA who is contacting others on your behalf. But the dialog and conversations after that have to be done by your Outreach leader directly. Once you need to have content written for other sites that will include links to yours, it needs to go to your writer.

Again, don't expect the same person to do all of this. They are all completely different skill sets.

Vendors

Sometimes, companies that understand how important it is to constantly have new people linking to them use vendors. There are many vendors that offer link building as a service. However, you have to be extremely careful. Most (not many: *most*) of these vendors are shady. They will offer the same "list" of sites that they can get links on for you to everyone else. So when Google sees that the links aren't actually editorial in nature and that anyone with a checkbook can purchase them, they lose their value.

What you're looking for in a link building vendor is a company that will look at the content your company has to link to (assets), and either use that as what we call "link bait" or help you to create some. The ideal vendor will then perform his or her own research, create specific contact lists for you, do the outreach, and organize and write all of the content.

Good vendors are expensive, but generally (based on our experience) will let you purchase links on some kind of an acquisition basis.

Managing these relationships is easy while they are performing well. However, the person in charge of them needs to be able to think on their feet and constantly be testing new vendors for quality and efficiency.

Research

One of the best ways to rank your site in the search engines is to know why Google has placed the sites that are at the top, well, at the top. Using Ahrefs.com, you can actually break out all of the pages on a competing site and find all of the links that are pointing to it. Additionally, you can look at all of the content on the site that is doing well socially.

We call these digital footprints and you can recreate them so easily.

Analysis

Everything is constantly being analyzed. You want to know when rankings fall, when competitors get a win, etc. Constant analysis is imperative to an SEO strategy. If you do it well, then create action plans and actually execute, you'll have huge wins and always rank at the top for the phrases you know will generate significant revenue for your organization.

PAID TRAFFIC

Paid traffic is just what it sounds like: traffic that is paid for, generally per click and lands on your site. There are social traffic channels as well as search traffic channels. There are also paid content traffic channels.

Depending on how large your organization is, you may have different people on the team that are experts in different paid traffic platforms. We have seen many people who are really solid when it comes to paid search traffic but struggle with paid social traffic.

Don't assume that all of them aren't needed because, as you learned earlier, even if you serve a B2B product or service, you can retarget the people who landed on your site from an email campaign or a paid search campaign with ads on Facebook. When you do, it's only the people who have searched for something and hit your site (or who have been sent an email by you and clicked through) who are seeing those ads.

You can also do a download from LinkedIn of people who are your perfect type of candidates and create an audience on Facebook, only targeting those individuals. It's incredibly powerful, and we've done it successfully hundreds of times for hundreds of companies.

There are many advanced strategies with all of these paid channels, but someone on your team needs to be responsible for making them a success.

Display Ads

If you sell a product that could be given out as a gift by companies to their employees, you can use display ads to advertise your product on pages that specifically talk about "the best corporate gifts for employees." So many people don't think outside the box, fail to target well with display ads, and then make the decision that display ads aren't effective for their business.

Like many of the concepts in this book, the tools are incredible. However, if you don't use them with your brain, you're going to be missing out on massive opportunities.

TECHNICAL DEVELOPMENT

One of the last things you need to hire full time in most companies, but that can create the highest impact tools for lead acquisition revolves around technical development.

This is also one of the most misunderstood areas.

Great technical development people in the marketing world have an eye for design as well as brilliance with code. Let's dig in a bit.

Site Development

Designers design. Developers develop. Think of it as the outside of a car looking great, but not being able to do anything if there's no engine. Developers literally create the engine and make sure it is constantly working.

We talked about SEO above, and how page speed is a really important part of making sure the SEO "t's are crossed" and "i's are dotted". The technical development team is going to be the ones to do this. The technical development team will actually make all of those calculators and tools work effectively. All the website-related stuff that doesn't focus on how it looks involves the technical development team.

Tracking

Everything your company does needs to be tracked so you know where your investment is and isn't getting you results. This tracking includes basic things like Google Analytics and more complicated things like Hotjar, CallRail scripts, Google Tag Manager and more. These tools, when used properly, allow you to see exactly what's happening and (most importantly) what's not working.

The technical development team will help you to ensure everything is tracked, but they need to be empowered by you to actually know what to put into place.

UI/UX Dev

Earlier, we talked about design's role in creating user interfaces and user experiences, but they can't handle it alone. The tech team is responsible to make sure that all of those things work well behind the scenes.

Server Optimization

Computers get "old." Ever get a computer that was the best on the market and then a few years later it started to lock up and run really slow? The servers that sites and apps run on are nothing more than computers, and they also get old. They need to be upgraded and software needs to be updated just like your home computer or laptop.

Your technical development team is the team responsible to make sure that all of those things are taken care of in a proactive way.

JOB DESCRIPTION EXAMPLE

In an effort to be as helpful as possible, I want to provide an example job description that we use to help qualify people. Obviously, as we are an agency, our job descriptions may differ from yours, but this will give you a good example to follow.

PAID TRAFFIC MANAGER JOB DESCRIPTION

Conklin Media is a fast-growing digital agency that helps companies across North America to grow, using highly defined and profit focused digital marketing strategies. These strategies often include creating paid traffic campaigns that send traffic from social media and search engines to assets designed by our team. We then create retargeting campaigns that push these individuals through a ProfitPath®, leading them to a conversion for our customers.

If you're a highly experienced paid traffic professional who can look at the big picture of a business growth strategy, create audiences in social media platforms, build profitable paid search campaigns, work with our visual media team to create amazing digital assets and ads, and then optimize and report on what you've done, we'd love to talk with you about joining our team of business growth strategists.

To be clear, we're not looking for just a "PPC Person" or a "Paid Facebook" person. We are looking for a business growth pro who understands and can explain how their suggested audiences, ad copy, and strategies will affect our client's desired business growth. We need someone who can look at the goal of a business, create a solid strategy based on research, and then execute on that strategy. We need someone who can strategize, create, and is tenacious about execution. Sound like a lot? It is.

We realize that this is a unique qualification. But we're looking for the few that exist.

What you'll be doing

Once a new client is brought on board, you'll attend a kick-off meeting where all of the goals will be discussed with our team and the client's team. During this meeting, the entire strategy will be discussed. As an example, this strategy could include:

1. A paid search campaign that sends search traffic to a landing page that's intended to "pixel" the visitors or create trackable phone calls.
2. Working with the design team to design ads and copy that will pull those people back to then use a calculator created by our dev team.
3. Using Zapier or Ontraport to automatically have the people who use the calculator added to a retargeting group on Facebook.
4. Building more audiences from scratch on Facebook to target cold traffic to the same original offer - and using ad spy tools to ensure we are creating ads and CTAs that have worked for others.
5. Speaking with clients on the phone about the results you have achieved and the vision for the future.

Throughout this process, no one will be holding your hand. It will be your responsibility to get client input, learn the client's best customers, and put yourself in the shoes of a potential buyer to create a great strategy that will get results.

We are looking for world-class talent.

Who you'll be working with

Our team is made up of experienced designers, coders, SEO Experts, business growth consultants, conversion optimization specialists, writers, and more. We've been doing this successfully for years. Our team is unique to the typical agency because we don't hire specialists. We hire what we call "**specializing generalists**."

This is why we're looking for someone who can build out landing pages, research keywords, create audiences, analyze analytics, give ideas on interactive content development, work with tracking codes, and manage vendor relationships.

Even though we need you to be experienced in all these areas, you'll be working with a team who overlaps in many of these areas as well, while focusing on their "general specialty."

Qualifications

We need someone with a massive resume. We aren't looking for an entry level individual for this position. We're going to expect you to be fast at what you do and incredibly focused on attention to detail. To succeed, you'll need to:

- Have an ability to understand the types of customers a business is looking to acquire and generate strategies, audiences, and keyword campaigns, and landing pages that help to facilitate that goal. Many times these businesses will have products, services, and models you have never heard of.

- Be comfortable with multitasking and working on many projects at once, switching gears regularly.
- Have a desire to collaborate with other experts on the team.
- Possess amazing attention to detail.
- Be a well-spoken and confident communicator that can clearly articulate business goals and objectives.
- Be a creative problem solver, possess a strong self-confidence, and have a natural ability to work under pressure.
- Have proven strong project management and time management skills.
- Have an advanced understanding of:
  - Paid search including Google, Yahoo, Bing, and second tier search
  - Paid social including Facebook, Instagram, LinkedIn, and new platforms as they come on the market and gain popularity.
  - User Experience as it relates to paid search quality scores, AMP, Facebook content, and more.
  - Split testing platforms such as VWO, Google Optimize, and others.
  - CRO Tools like Hotjar
  - Google Analytics, Google Tag Manager, etc.
- Have a strong desire to learn and get better. You'll be responsible for self-educating on new strategies, new platforms, etc.
- Constantly increase your efficiency by demoing new tools, and staying on top of the industry.
- Be passionate about and have a desire and capability to successfully make decisions independently and confidently.

- Possess a desire to learn new software and strategies being used in the market.
- Be able to travel a few weeks out of the year, if need be.

It is REQUIRED that you have at least 4 years of experience creating paid traffic strategies for businesses and executing on those strategies. It will be important for us to see REAL examples.

Compensation & Benefits

Health Insurance

Our company provides fully paid health coverage for every full time employee. Additional family members may be added at the expense of the employee.

Unlimited Time Off

We have an "unlimited time off" policy, which means that if you need time off, take time off. However, this doesn't mean that the work doesn't get done. Our team members are mature and dedicated enough that when they are going to be out of town, they proactively ensure that nothing on their plate is dropped.

Zero Tolerance Gossip Policy

We are dedicated to having an environment where people don't speak negatively about each other behind their backs. We define gossip as "saying something negative about someone else on the team to a person who can't fix the situation." In other words, if you have a concern, speak with your supervisor about it, or address it directly with the person in question.

Profit Sharing

When our team helps to create profit, we believe in sharing it. Our profit sharing is distributed quarterly, and you'll find us to be more transparent than most companies about our numbers. The calculations for profit sharing are generally based on longevity and seniority, so the longer you're on our team, the better.

Work From Home Wednesdays

Some of our team members choose to work from home on Wednesdays from time to time. While the office is still open, this is a time for you to focus on projects that you can more effectively handle outside of the office, or simply to get a change of scenery.

There may be times when your supervisor will require you to be in the office on Wednesdays.

Would you like to apply?

If you meet the requirements here, please send an email to hello@conklinmedia.com along with your resume and why you think you're the perfect fit. We can't wait to hear from you!

Continued Training

I have a feeling that I'll be writing a book specifically on ProfitPaths® in the future, but based on how long it took me to put this one together, I assume it's going to be awhile.

But here's something awesome. As I write this, we already have the content ready in the early lessons of a course we created for ProfitPaths®. You can find a link to the course at LostAt30k.com.

We aren't sure how we're going to price the courses yet, but as an owner of this book, I've decided to post the transcripts below to the first course, which is an introduction to ProfitPaths®. I hope you find it valuable!

One last thing, you can also find a link to a webinar that talks about the course at LostAt30k.com. The webinar is totally free and gives you a high level of ProfitPaths® so you can make sure it's something you'd like to learn more about before spending money on the course.

Enjoy the transcripts below!

PROFITPATH® OVERVIEW & FOUNDATION COURSE TRANSCRIPTS

How It Came To Be (LESSON TRANSCRIPT - PLEASE PARDON GRAMMATICAL AND SPELLING ERRORS)

Hi there, it's Dave Conklin, I'm so excited that you're hanging out with me to do this overview video of ProfitPaths®, how it all came to be, and how it all started. This is my home office. Some of these videos are going to be from my home office. Some will be from my office at the corporate office. Sometimes I might even do some videos outside or from different spots in my office here. It just depends on the situation. You'll get to see all kinds of stuff throughout the course.

The goal of what we're going to talk about right now is just to give you kind of the background story of how this came to be, because it has a lot to do with the reason it's been so successful. It was created to solve a problem originally, and it wasn't even called ProfitPaths® when it launched. So let's go back in time, about 20 years. Pop quiz, can you remember what video this is from? Might show your age a little bit. It's Back to the Future with Michael J. Fox. So we're gonna go back in time. I get out of real estate (or I get out of high school, excuse me). I want to go into real estate. And the reason I want to go into real estate is because I knew that selling houses was a great opportunity to make some money if you could sell enough of them, because that's the most expensive thing you can sell, pretty much. Unless you're into some kind of nuclear products or something like that that you're moving (selling).

So I was I was so excited to get into this business, but I didn't know anybody. I was in my early 20s. I didn't have a big network of people.

There was only one thing that I could do to generate this business. And that was cold call. Now you're saying, wait a minute, there's a lot of other stuff that you can do. Yeah, but I had a really focused effort on helping people who wanted to SELL a house. The reason for that is if I could find people that were selling a house, they would also be buying a house most likely. So I'd be able to get a commission on both deals, which means I can make twice as much money if I'm working on someone who wasn't just buying a house. I really wanted to focus on those sellers. I knew also that if I sold a $115,000 house, I would make a commission that was approximately $3,400. But if I sold a house that was $615,000, I could make an $18,000 commission. So why would I focus my efforts on the small one rather than the large one? This meant I had to actually find homes that were more expensive. All of this comes into play in just a little bit and you're going to understand how this all relates back to the whole ProfitPaths® concept. So the $615,000 house is found in specific neighborhoods, generally. So what did I do? I drove around to different neighborhoods all over my area and I found ones that had these really expensive houses in them. Then, I wrote down all of the different street addresses and things like that. Now, I want you to stop for a second before I go on to talk in deeper.

I want you to write down your highest profit products and services and the very specific buyer that would buy those services, because that is a foundation for how all of this works.

We're going to cover this in a little bit more detail in future videos. But this is really important for you to understand. Now, I want to give you an example. I was speaking at an event and I think it was Vancouver, Canada or something like that, B.C. and there was an LED lighting provider there. I asked him, "what is your what is your biggest potential customer?".

And he said, "Well, we sell LCD lights. So, you know, wealthier homeowners that want to have, like, you know, street lights put in or something and got into their driveway. That's a big client for us.".

I said, "OK. Did they buy the highest volume of product from you?" And he was like, "No. Townships and municipalities do.".

And I said, "Okay. Who's the individual?".

"Their road masters."

I said, "So are you telling me that if you can if you can market specifically to road masters of these different townships and boroughs, that you can sell really high dollar and high quantity LED streetlights to them for a really high profit. And it's probably your probably your most profitable customer?".

"Absolutely," he said.

"So that is your ProfitPath®."

Selling this specific product to this specific individual. We're gonna go into that in a little bit more detail. Now, I realized that I had this very specific avatar that I wanted to go after and we're going to go over these avatar sheets later. So I created these this plan that really broke out all these different examples. And we're going to go over that in future videos as well. But getting back to the foundation, I wanted to help people that were selling these high dollar houses. So I went back and I got this thing called the reverse phone directory. Now, the reverse phone directory is like a phone book, if you remember those. You would open it up and it was ordered by zip code first. Then you could page through and it had the street names in alphabetical order. And then you could look and you could see every single home in the street and you could call them. I had all these street names written down have these really expensive houses? So I'd start cold calling and I had a tremendous amount of success cold calling. Until the roller coaster happened.

Now, if you've been in sales or you've ever done sales training, you know that you have to fill the top of the funnel with leads, with prospects. I had to call people and those phone calls when I called them and I said, "hey, my name's Dave. I work in the area in real estate. I'm looking to build out my real estate portfolio. Some I'm calling people on your street today to see if anybody's looking to make a move in the next six months or so. Out of every 200 phone calls, generally, I'd get a "yes." I'd go meet with them. I'd list the house and then I'd start my work.

Now, the problem is, once I had a lot of work and a lot of business, I couldn't cold call anymore. So now the top of the funnel wasn't getting filled and I didn't have a network to go and refer business. So I was in a really rough situation and I knew that I had to do something to stop this roller coaster from preventing my financial stability to be where it needed to be. Now, stop for a second and take action again. I want you to write down what channels or markets you're currently depending on to generate new business.

This is so important. There's different situations where we've had many different things, I'll talk about in just a second, that went away and it prevented us from growing and in some cases actually made us lose revenue in a in a big, big way.

Could those things go away?

Could a partnership that you currently have that you're getting a lot of business from go away?

Is there an employee that happens to have a really large Rolodex? Could that go away?

Could that specific billboard that you've been buying for years go away?

Could a street be put in that moves traffic from your current, you know, traffic pattern that's benefiting you to somewhere else? Could that go away?

This is a risk analysis because ProfitPaths® help you to avoid that risk. Now, other examples would be cold calling, which was my case. If cold calling goes away, I've got a huge problem.

Google, if you remember the penguin update (one of the worst in my memory) where you had all these Web sites that were foundationally built the way that Google felt that it wanted them to be built. Then Google changed their mind about how it looked at a lot of the sites that it was currently giving credit for, and it went away completely.

How about Facebook? If you're a publisher, or you've ever had a Facebook group that had like a million people, or a million followers, and all the sudden you're posting content one day and none of the followers are seeing it. That is a huge issue.

Or, maybe there's a specific market. Now, in my particular case, it was the real estate market from 2007 to 2009. It annihilated our company. And you'll learn about that in a little bit.

So, I had to create leads in a way that didn't depend on my time. That was this really big focus that I had. So, I'm like, "I know! I'm going to make a Web site! I'm going to create a Web site in all my problems are going to be solved!" So in early 2000, I built this sucker. Now, let me tell you something, this was hot back in the day. But it didn't generate any leads at all. It didn't generate one call. It didn't generate one e-mail.

And not one person filled out the form. It was super frustrating to me. I was banging my head against the wall like this guy.

(I don't know what this is from, by the way. It's one of those maybe it's. I don't know. Anyway, it doesn't matter).

But the point is that I was very frustrated. And I know for a fact that I'm not alone. Many people, even today, in the 2020's, we still have people who are building these Web sites and putting them out there. They're literally not doing a thing. And it's horrible. It's because they're not focused on the profit path methodology.

So even with all the incredibly helpful ads that are out there, 78 percent of businesses are still not satisfied with their conversions on their Web site, according to HubSpot. But why? Well, it's because we're not focusing on the solutions. And that's what this is all about.

This is My Friends business, who owns a septic pumping company. And he focuses on the specific thing that people want when they're looking to get their septic tank pumped. You know what it is? How much is it? And you know what? You can only get this deal at our local fair that he offers to people. They know that when they go there, they're going to sign up right then and there. They're going to pay and they're going to get a special price that they will not get anywhere else or any other time during the year. They're providing a very specific solution to a very specific audience. Who? People who attend the local fair? Now, what's the fair pumping special? How much is it? Well, you have to go to the booth to find out. So it's the same thing. In my case, people buying or selling a house, my website didn't work because it wasn't focusing specifically on what they wanted. And what they wanted was to know how much they can sell their house for. It's incredibly important to know how much you can then afford to purchase in your new home or what can you afford to pay off when you sell that house. So we built this site:.

It was called GMHV and, over the years it generated millions of leads for about ten thousand different agents and it turned into an actual company on itself. And from this lesson, we learned that solution based marketing, not marketing your brand or your company. Marketing, a very specific focused solution, to a very specific focused audience generates results online. Over and over and over again in all kinds of different industries. So ProfitPaths® is all about how to take your company and brand, market, and sell very specific focused solutions – for very specific audiences. It's become a part of our DNA completely. This whole entire idea. Now, what happened in my world was we had the real estate market go up and then it crashed so aggressively. And it really hurt a lot.

So then we launched our agency. We started doing the same exact things for a few hundred other companies and continues to do so throughout the years. And today we call it ProfitPaths®. I'm so excited that you're going to be learning about it with us through these different videos.

We're going to talk in this next video about how and why ProfitPaths® actually work. We're going to dove into some really specific examples and then we're going to talk about the things that you're going to need to actually make ProfitPaths® a success. Then we're going to talk about finding talent, because chances are with all the stuff that you have to do within this ProfitPath® system, in this framework, you probably don't currently have the talent in-house. But if you do, you're going to realize it and you're going to know it. And then at the end, you'll get to take your quiz. We'll get to see how many of these different things you actually remember. Then, we'll get you a score so that you know how well you did.

I can't wait to see in the next video.

How & Why ProfitPaths® Work For Potential Customers (LESSON TRANSCRIPT - PLEASE PARDON GRAMMATICAL AND SPELLING ERRORS)

Hey, it's Dave Conklin. I'm excited to talk about how and why ProfitPaths® actually work. In this video, we're going to talk about why it works really well for the consumer side. In the next video, we'll talk about why it works really well for businesses to utilize to help them grow.

So consumers, when they have a challenge, have some kind of a desire or a need that they need to have a solution for. It would make complete sense to you, I assume, if in one example, we would go and have a lot of different paths that we have to go down in order to find that solution and get that result that we want. On the other side, if there's a second option where we have a straight line to a solution, psychologically, that just feels better. That's exactly what ProfitPaths® do. Because we're creating specific assets, meaning white paper downloads, online tools, different resources like that. For an individual who has a very specific problem or challenge or desire, we're providing them with a straight line that makes them feel confident and excited that you will actually have that specific solution for them.

The messaging and the voice that we create with these ProfitPaths® are going to be ones that ring true to the person that's in that specific situation. I'll give you an example. I'm just off the top of my head thinking swimming pools. Let's say, for example, that you have a pool company. You could just market your pool company and pool company services and things like that. But let's say there's a really high profit dollar per transaction (not percentage necessarily), but a very high profit dollar amount that you actually get when you do, we'll call it, "chlorine remediation," going in and helping a customer to fix some of their chlorine challenges that they're having.

Well, you can create a Web site, for example, called FixMyChlorine.com. When that person goes to Google and they search for things like "how to lower chlorine levels," or "how to fix chlorine levels," and they come across a Web site that directly speaks to their problem, their challenge that they have, and all of the solutions on that site are all about that specific challenge and problem. That's really exciting for them. They feel like they've found a home as opposed to just pulling up the local pool manufacturing company and looking them up online. So that's the voice in the messaging. We really create stuff that's so focused.

It may even be someone who's at a certain type of business in a certain industry and they have a certain job title. Because they work in that industry and they have that job title, they probably have certain needs. For example, a plant manager might want to increase the workplace safety ratings. Well, you might have a manufacturing consulting company that helps people to do that as one of your products or services. Again, by hitting ads to that specific individual while they're going through and looking up something that has to do with that topic of workplace safety. Well, when you have these ads that come up that don't brand your company and talk about your company, but they actually brand a white paper or a tool or some information or a study on focused content around workplace safety in a plant, and they download it because it's actually of interest to them – and it provides value. Now you know they downloaded it. Now you can start to market your solution to them, because they've identified by downloading that content.

We're getting a little bit into the next video. But to the to the consumer, the psychology is so spot on because you're focusing exclusively on them with direct solutions to their problem and their desire.

So, we want to get people from the left to the right. And we want to do it in the easiest way possible for them. And ProfitPaths® are a great solution. So that's how and why they work for the customer.

Let's talk in the next video about how and why they work for you, the business.

HOW & WHY PROFITPATHS® WORK FOR BUSINESS GROWTH (LESSON TRANSCRIPT - PLEASE PARDON GRAMMATICAL AND SPELLING ERRORS)

Hey, it's Dave again.

We're going to talk about how ProfitPaths® benefits you as a business. There are so many different things that come into play when you start to use the ProfitPaths® methodology to build out your business growth initiatives. You might be experiencing one of these emotions. If you're not, know that many people are around the globe when they're doing digital marketing, budget planning, and things like that in their organization. They're either angry or they're confused. We hear it every day. People are so frustrated with digital marketing agencies because they're giving them metrics like "video views" and "Facebook likes" and all these things. None of that actually puts money in their bank account.

The only metric that really, truly matters to them is profit. And you may feel the same way.

Well, this anger comes from empty promises that are being made and things like that. It's happening because many people are going about doing things in a way that's completely illogical and doesn't allow any detailed tracking.

The problem that the marketers have (because some marketers do want to do it right), is that the executives are frustrated already. They've been tainted by bad experiences. Therefore, the executives don't want to give the freedom to the marketers because they don't really understand how it all works. Some are just confused because they see these amazing metrics. They see that their Facebook page gets all this traction and traffic, but it's not translating into customers.

The ProfitPaths® methodology fixes all of that.

The first thing it does is allow you to create new streams of revenue using current business products and services. And it's all completely trackable. You can take a ProfitPath® and all the money you invest and the revenue that comes from it and track everything. It's so trackable, because of how it's established and set up, that you could actually create a separate P&L in Quickbooks or whatever accounting software you use. You could use classes or many different things. This isn't an accounting class, but you could have a separate P&L created specifically for this because the products and services you're going to move will come from this channel, which is completely trackable back to the beginning.

The second thing, it gives you market change protection. So instead of focusing on one big marketing campaign for your company overall, you're going to have all these micro ProfitPaths® running that each are responsible for their own revenue. Even though it's certainly possible that many of those different channels could be affected by a negative market change or a change in the industry all at the same time, you can create different ProfitPaths® that are unrelated to each other in terms of industry or product. That creates an insurance policy of sorts so you'll still have revenue coming in should one of the other channels disintegrate.

The third thing, it allows you to create a new and sellable entity. You're actually creating an asset for your business that could be sellable to one of your potential competitors, or maybe somebody who's not really a competitor but is interested in your market, or in marketing to the same client base that your ProfitPath® has established. There are so many opportunities.

For example, we worked with a manufacturing company that had very large jigsaws. They were having a market downturn in the area where they sold some of the custom cut wood pieces they created with these jigsaws. So, they used their same technology to create puzzles. Large scale photo puzzles the size of a wall. They created a web site specifically focused on those puzzles, and they sold a lot of puzzles. While that was completely separate, they used the same equipment, same resources. Because it was completely separate from the industry that was harmed in a really negative way, they still had revenue.

And the last thing, it provides clarity. So CEOs, CFO's, they all want to know what is the money we're spending actually creating in revenue back. Setting things up with the ProfitPaths® methodology allows you to understand from start to finish exactly what's happening with the money and how much money is actually being generated from it. So those are some of the reasons why ProfitPath® is so great for your business.

I hope this was helpful to you and we'll see you in the next video.

Examples of Success (LESSON TRANSCRIPT - PLEASE PARDON GRAMMATICAL AND SPELLING ERRORS)

Before we get into anything further, I think it's really important that you see a couple of examples of ProfitPaths®. And just to start off, we're going to start off with our own. So ironically, the very course that you're taking right now, this ProfitPath® course is a ProfitPath® in itself. This course is designed to help companies that don't necessarily either have the type of budget it takes to have us build a ProfitPath® or CEOs who want their team to understand the concept of ProfitPaths® and learn about it, or just people that want to make themselves better marketers by adding some additional ideas to their toolset. So we created this ProfitPath® specifically for those purposes. We have some other tools and things like that, such as CEO know where we actually create software that's affordable for people that they can go and learn more about their company's marketing and where they're at. But it's geared to the CEO so they can stay up to date on how their team is doing with their internal marketing. Now, these are different assets or different ProfitPaths® that allow us to bring people into our business in separate ways and build relationships with them.

So let's go a little bit more brick and mortar. This example is an awning company out of the Detroit area. They decided to create a ProfitPath® for themselves with a company called Auto Floor Guard. They used a lot of their relationships with vendors for materials and things. And we were able to create a completely separate entity altogether that generates revenue, but yet it still uses those existing vendor relationships that we talk about so often.

These are some of the videos that we created specifically for them. I'll show them to you now.

[VIDEO PLAYS]

So that's just an example of an asset that we created specifically to bring people into this particular ProfitPath®. Now, once they've seen the information, and winter time rolls around, we play this video to the same group of people.

[VIDEO PLAYS].

So there's a spring one and they go on and on.

This is another great example that we really love. It's a company in the flooring industry. They came to us and said, "look, we really want to sell our stuff digitally.".

"OK, cool. So what can you sell nationwide?"

And they said, "oh, well, carpet tiles!"

"Perfect. Who buys the highest volume of carpet tiles?" we asked.

"Churches and universities.".

We said, "Awesome. We'll start with churches.".

So we created a marketing campaign specifically targeting pastors and other leaders at churches with this carpet tile website called Divinity Floors. We built content all around pastors and things of interest to them. So it created a completely separate revenue channel for their existing business. It's just a really good example. And this is a video that we made that if you reach out to us, we can show that to you. For time's sake, don't do it now.

So another example. This company wanted to rank and Google for a lot of terms like "executive search firms," "best executive search firms," and "top executive search firms." And they wanted to take that organic traffic and market their own business. The people who are interested in an executive search firm are the very people that they want to talk to.

We created a Web site geared toward rating the best executive search firms in the country. We got it ranking extremely well because it was a list in itself and we allowed some of the people that were in on the list to put badges on their Web site that promoted the search firm site and made it rank really well on Google. Google is not going to show any kind of bias or preference by having a company's Web site rank at the top for a specific term like that. But in this case, it was one of the only ranking sites out there. So it ranked really quickly and really well. Today it enjoys a ton of traffic around that topic. The company that started it is then able to generate revenue by retargeting the traffic that goes to that Web site.

Here's another example, a tech firm that has a lot of different products and services for a lot of different audiences. We created a Web site, a microsite that was geared specifically toward helping CFO's and CIO's at extremely large companies get a free trial of what is otherwise a really expensive software package, that's also really complicated to set up. This company will even set it up for them. So it's one of those things where a lot of these companies want to do this, but it's just going to take too much money and too much manpower to make it happen. So what they do is what they did with us is we came and created a list. We market that particular solution to a lot of different people and we experience a lot of wins for them.

Another example is an industrial valve repair company. They came to us and said, "Hey, we want to target chemical plants and oil refineries. Those two industries. So we created a Web site specifically geared toward those audiences and created content around those audiences. The reason we did that is that we wanted those people to know that we know what we're doing at chemical plants and oil refineries. And so we tracked the phone numbers. We do content on LinkedIn specifically to the audience of people that hire those valve repair specialists. And that's been a big win.

This is a really great success story. Woodtex is a storage shed company and they noticed that they were getting a lot of traction with their log cabins. So they decided that they were going to build a ProfitPath®, focused specifically on cabins. We created an entirely new design of the Woodtex Web site. The River Wood Cabins site is separate and we've been able to help them to generate an incredible amount of business and sell a lot of cabins all across the country. it's all based on this idea of separating out a brand or an entity or a specific need or desire that customers have and going with just that brand. Now they have two entities that are completely separate that generate separate revenue.

One of the last examples I'm going to use is, is this one. This is a glass company, but they decided they wanted to get into the sunroom game. So we created them a very simple lead generation page focused on generating leads only for sunrooms and it generates leads at about $76 a pop. They'll sell one out of five or so and they make around $20,000 per sale, generally speaking. So it's a great, great, great turnover, a whole new form of leads for their sales team.

This is a company that sells on memory cards on Amazon and we built for them bulk memory cards dot com, because they wanted to sell their memory cards in a way that would be completely exclusive from Amazon because Amazon could wake up one day, snap their fingers and it's gone. So we helped them to be able to do that. But we couldn't build a site just for memory cards. We had to go the bulk route. So when we looked at these different keywords and what people are searching for, we discover that there were a lot of people looking up wholesale and bulk memory cards. We launched the site specifically geared toward that. And today, if you Google Bulk or wholesale memory cards, you'll see them right at the top. The organic part of Google.

So it's important to understand as well that ProfitPaths® are for every single stage of the buying, upselling and referral phases. You can warm an audience up using the ProfitPath® methodology. You can close deals using it. You can generate referrals. The reason that this is so important to understand is that some people get it in their heads that a ProfitPath® is the same every time. ProfitPaths® is a methodology. It's taking your product or service that is really high profit; matching it up with your highest, most successful order per sale type of customer, and creating content and assets to market to them in a way that positions you as the expert, the person to go to.

Those are some examples of ProfitPaths®.

There's a lot more! So if you'd like to have more, you can email us at hello@conklinmedia.com and let us know that you'd like to see some additional examples.

Also, if you have questions at this point like, "Well, hold on – what kind of ProfitPath® can I build for my business?".

Just go ahead and send us an email to hello@conklinmedia.com and we'll do our best to brainstorm with you a bit. See you in the next video!

THINGS YOU'RE GOING TO NEED (LESSON TRANSCRIPT - PLEASE PARDON GRAMMATICAL AND SPELLING ERRORS)

Hey, it's Dave with Conklin Media. Welcome to the portion of our training where we talk about the things that you're going to need in order to build a successful ProfitPath® campaign. We're going to be speaking mostly about tools and worksheets and things like that.

This is the very first one, the ProfitPaths® planning worksheet.

This becomes really helpful in actually breaking down the specific things that you're going to be able to market to which audiences. The first page of this ProfitPaths® planning sheet is where you actually break down your products and your services that have the highest profit dollar per sale. The reason you want to focus on those things first is that in your company there are products and services you offer that are likely more favorable to the bottom line. So if you think of it as a revenue silo, we want to start with products that are going to have a big impact on you. Then, you continue to build new ProfitPaths® in your business so that each one creates a new stream of revenue. It's just logical that you would start with the ones that have the highest revenue per sale, not percentage revenue per sale. That causes a lot of confusion when we talk about this.

The example that I have here is a company that sells different equipment for warehouses. One of the things that they sell is electric forklifts. They make an average profit per customer of about $4,300. On this worksheet, you're going to want to actually break all of that down. Now, we're going to go into this in much more detail in a future training video.

But over here is where you talk about the following. The warehouse managers in Vancouver, for this particular example, are the people who would most likely be the purchasers of these $4,300 profit per sale electric forklifts. Over here we break down what social networks are they on? Are those people on Facebook looking at pictures of their grandkids and things? Are they actually using linked in? Are they on YouTube? And then you'll just indicate which networks there. It just helps with some of the brainstorming. So then down below here, we get into the resources of interest to them. For example, these are warehouse managers in Vancouver (that's your avatar) and when they're in the market for electric forklifts. What resources might those people find to be interesting? An example we came up with here is a "long term cost savings case study of electric versus gas forklifts." That's the example of a resource we could create for them in different situations. I gave in an earlier video, an example of a flooring company that is marketing carpet tiles and things like that to pastors. Well, we did a lot of resources for that particular audience on how to raise money for your church, because if they're currently in the middle of doing a building project in their church where they may need carpet tiles, we want to make sure that we're providing those pastors with something to get the conversation started. It's like dating, which we're going to go over in just a second. You can't just hit them over the head immediately with "buy my stuff." That's what everybody does. Nobody wants that. We're building a relationship using content with them. That's what ProfitPaths® is all about. Creating a specific avatar that we want to target, providing them with a lot of helpful resources while branding what we do. Then once they are ready to actually make that buying decision, they raise their hand and they say, "You know what? This is a company that we felt confident in providing this solution for us.

Then we break down what kind of delivery method can we use for this particular resource? So using the example of a long term cost savings case study of electric versus gas forklifts, we could create a PDF on that that people could download and give us their email to build an email list. We could create a video that we could put in front of pastors while they're surfing around YouTube and other video platforms. We could create an article that we get published on some external Web sites like sermons.com or whatever. This is a bad example, obviously, because I just mixed the church stuff with the forklift stuff. So Thomasnet.com or some other place that a lot of these warehouse managers are going online. Then we talk about what stage is this appropriate to hit that content within? Is this when they really are hot for us, so to speak, and that dating relationship? Are they really are confident in us at this point? Have they seen a lot of stuff already from us? Or is this something where we can actually hit people while they're still cold and don't even know who we are? So that's what this page 1 of this worksheet is all about.

The second page is where we really break down this process of attracting a stranger and we talk about what resources we can use.

- When they become a visitor and actually know who we are, what kind of content can we use to convert them?
- Then to get those leads that we've converted into a closing situation, what kind of content can we push there?
- Once they become customers, how do we turn them into promoters and actually get us to or get them to talk about us to their friends?
- Then we break down different communication channels.

So the first thing you're going to need, without a doubt, are these ProfitPaths®, planning sheets, and they're available for download in the resource section below.

The next thing you'll need is our example plans.

We use something called lucid chart for this stuff and this is where we break everything like the research and data for this avatar, the product, and service we're going to move, what kind of research have we done that shows that people are actually looking for this stuff? And then is there data online where stuff is available? Then we go into the awareness section identifying what tools online are we going to use to make people aware like google search ads, cold e-mail, digital PR, Facebook and Instagram ads, display ads, YouTube ads, and we talk about how we're actually going to go about marketing to those people.

Then our assets section breaks out what content are we going to create. So in this case, we're creating a viral video, a white paper, some ego bait, a raise cash tool, an idea slideshow, and a crowdfunding resource that they can use. Then what are we going to actually do to convert them? So what's it going to look like? What are we building?

When you do a sheet like this, it gives everyone on your team clarity as to what specifically we are building together. So the designer, the copywriter, the programmer, the link building person who does that digital PR, and your paid traffic people; they're all on the same page and they know exactly what we're building. So this example plan is really helpful. Now we're actually redesigning that right now to look more like this.

We're going to be creating a new way to lay all that out. Here's the sneak peek of our new logo. At this point in time, we're not currently marketing this. But as we solidify it more and more, we're going to be able to do that. We also have some software coming out that's going to help you to drag and drop and build one of these on your own. So those are the worksheets that you're going to need.

There's a couple of tools that we highly recommend.

One of them, for example, is SpyFu.

Spyfu is great because it allows you to see what your competitors are currently doing from a paid traffic perspective. So just as an example, if

I come in here and I put in a Web site like bed tester dot com, we can actually see who the competitors are to that site. So you'd put one of your competitors in here, find one that's spending money currently on clicks, and you can go down and see some that are really doing a lot. So cocoon by Sealy, you can see here, there they're buying about $13,000 per month in traffic on Google paid. We can look down here and we can see the keyword phrases that they're currently purchasing, about how many impressions they're getting, and how many other competitors are buying them. Then we can also see something really powerful, and we can see what keyword phrases they're purchasing. We can also see what they're actually buying. So, for example, they're a competitor to Casper Mattresses. They're buying the phrase "Casper mattress." Their ad copy is "don't buy the hype, save hundreds on Cocoon." So they're actually using a competitor's keyword to buy this traffic. So this tool is going to allow you to do is look at people in the industry who are currently trying to do what you're doing and you're going to get to see stuff. Now, some of you are like, well, mattresses are common. You know, what other stuff can we look at? Well, if we go in here and instead of this one, we do something. Really? Really. So, Thomasnet.net Is like a manufacturing type company. You can see here that they're not actually doing a lot on the paid side. So you might have that come up, where you dig in and there's nothing there. But we're going to show you in later videos how you can do research and you can find competitors that are doing things that are in your industry and you can have a huge win.

If I type in the word "gerotor", which you probably have never heard of (it's something that's actually found in your vehicle) I want to show you, there are 1,400 people a month typing in the phrase "gerotor pump." When we dig in here and we see a lot of keyword phrases that we're finding. These are things you probably have never heard of if you're not in this industry. And the reason I'm showing this to you is so you understand that it gets really specific. If you are in that market and we see that monthly power here is spending about three thousand a month on paid search, we can dig into them. And here's their keyword phrase. So if you sell these Rockford power take off or truck power take off or PTO power. I mean, I don't even know what these are. We can click on these and see the ads are that they're running and who else is running these ads? All these crazy data are available in spyfu. There is a link below where you can start spyfu and we may on some of the links below, just so you know, we may get a commission if you do purchase those because we have relationships with many of these different companies.

So the next one is Buzz Sumo.

When we develop a lot of the assets that we create for our customers, we start with Buzz Sumo to find content that's working really well. So I typed in the phrase "kitchen design" here; under their web analyzer. When you go to content and click "web" you'll see this. I then just typed in "kitchen design" just to show you an example. If you want to create some content or a resource or an asset (those are kind of the same things in many cases), you want to create something that is time tested. Something we know will go over really well. You can see the "top 50 most beautiful kitchen designs for 2019" here. That content has 39,000 Facebook engagements. So a lot of people have liked this. And we can actually click it and we can go to that Web site and we can see what they created that people like so stinking much. We can make sure that if we're in that kitchen design space, that we can create something even better so that when we offer it to people to download, they're going to like it on Facebook and they're going to want to download that content.

The next thing you're going to want is Google Analytics.

Google Analytics allows you to take a look at all of the traffic that's coming into your Web site. You can see where the traffic is coming from, where you're conversions are coming from, and all of the things we're going to talk about in a few moments you can track. These include clicks of a button and phone calls that come into your business from your Web efforts. You can track literally everything like the time on-site that people spend when they come from Facebook versus Pinterest versus that trade journal that you happen to advertise on. You can see all of that in the back end. You can also test things in real-time, which is incredibly important because right now on this particular site, you can see that no one is here. But just as an example, one of the other clients that we work with is (not in this account, of course.)...

I'm going to go in my screen over here and I'm going to actually go to online stamp dot net to show you how powerful this is. So I just loaded that up and as long as my IP address isn't blocked, you're going to see a visitor. So there I am. And you can see that I'm on the home page. And if you go to traffic sources, you can see that there was it was a direct source, meaning I just type directly in. But if I go to Google first and I type in online stamp dot net and I click on that link. So there's that. And you can see that that source came from Google because I Googled it first.

What I'm trying to show you is this. When you launch a new campaign to a new asset (so a new landing page, you create for a download, for example) and you start buying clicks and buying traffic. This allows you to actually in real-time watch how the traffic is coming in and how it's performing. You can see the conversions right away and know, "Is this working? Is it not working? What keywords are they typing in different things like that?" And that's really important. Google Analytics takes this real-time data. But then it also stores it so that you can do big analysis, so if you make a big change or something like that, you can go in and see if that change had a positive impact or not. Those changes could be anything from changing a button color to trying to increase conversions and you can test it. If you're ranking for a new keyword inside of Google paid you can then see if that keyword is going to have the same conversion rates as another one. There's a lot that you can do in analytics and it's really a must-have.

The tool you need is Ahrefs.

Ahrefs allows you to do a lot of things. One of those things is helping you to track the number of referring domains that are linking to you. Once you have a ProfitPath® where you're paying for traffic to land on a page, and after you pay for that traffic to land on that page, you see that there are successful conversions. You can see that that keyword phrase means money. Then you're going to want to go after what we call SEO or search engine optimization. That tactic makes your page rank in Google for the same or similar phrases to the ones that you've been paying for. So now you'll be getting that traffic for free after you have success with SEO, instead of having to pay per click to Google. Links from other Web sites that are pointing into your Web site are what increases those rankings. As those links come in, typically speaking, if your content is great, your Web site will rank higher in Google. And this is where you track all those things that are happening. So we can click on backlinks inside of this site and we can see where people are talking about us online...

So here's a page that apparently started linking to them in 2017, and then if we go back to here, we can see "that ultimate home." You can see this is a link that they apparently put up in 2019 that they you know, there's the link that clicks through and it goes here. You can see their article on this organization and things like that. So that's what this link tracking allows you to do. Now, Ahrefs allows you to do a lot more. You can also audit your Web site to see if there are issues with speed. You can track keywords. You can do something similar to BuzzSumo by looking at different content that works. There's a lot this can do. We're going to be using this tool in future videos, but you're going to want to have Ahrefs.

So the next thing would be SEMrush.

Now, SEMRush is a tool where we can track keywords. You can do this in Ahrefs as well. If you can only afford one, I would recommend Ahrefs because it's a little bit more robust and it's much better on the link building side and tracking that, and it still does the keywords and things. I just like the visual interface of SEMrush a little bit better. It's a little more friendly. We can go in here and see, if we're doing our job well, from an SEO perspective, this blue line is going to be going up into the right. That's always our goal. And you can see here we've had a lot of success with this client, for example. You can track the keyword phrases that are ranking for your site that may not be showing up in some of the analytics tools, because of the fact that they aren't actually generating traffic just yet as they aren't on the first page of Google. So this breakdown shows that the pages that rank really as well as the keyword phrases that rank extremely well. You can click this link (this is one thing I love to do) and we can see the pages that have the most keywords ranking. Here you can find different opportunities and stuff that you can take advantage of. So this is again, a really great tool to use.

Then we have Hotjar.

Hotjar has a really great interface where you can look at recordings of people that have been on your site. So let's just play this one, for example. This is an actual user who visited one of our clients. And you can see they came here and you can see they were trying to scroll to the right. They were on a mobile device. You can see they're trying to click on that. So this is a great example. Now they successfully scrolled over. So they're looking at this cable cover organization Kit on their phone and this is what they're doing while they're there. This is amazing to look at content like this as you're sending traffic for the first time to start to see how people are seeing it, how they're interacting with it. It can be incredibly beneficial.

It will also then take a heat map of all the traffic and show how far people are typically scrolling. Is there a hot area that their mouses staying over because people read with their mouse? What kind of data can we pull from this to further benefit our conversions and things like that? So you can see this person was here and they looked around for quite a long time.

So then there's CallRail.

CallRail allows you to do a couple of things that involve tracking your calls that come in off your Web site. It can actually work with your Google Analytics account so that you can see what traffic sources you're sending that are creating phone calls. If you have an ad running on a placemat, for example, you can put one phone number and then it'll actually dynamically generate phone numbers for traffic that comes from Google paid and Google organic search traffic. You didn't always have the ability to track the phone calls that come into your company from your Web site in the past. But today, you can do all of that. So you want those calls to count as a lead so you can have conversions fire in analytics to actually show, for example, "this keyword phrase generated 15 calls that lasted this amount or longer, whereas this keyword didn't generate any calls." You can then do some analysis and make sure that what you're doing is working.

The last thing is Mailchimp.

You have to have a tool that you're utilizing to make sure that your rankings and your traffic and all that are generating emails. You need a place for those e-mails to go that you can easily follow up with people. Mailchimp and others like constant contact and may others allow you to create an email drip campaign so that once somebody comes in and they sign up for a white paper or whatever, they then get added to a drip campaign and get followed up with. And that's one of the most effective forms of marketing that you can do.

So there are a lot of other tools as well. But these are the primary ones that we recommend that you have. If you had one tool only, it would be Google analytics for your tracking, which is free, by the way. And then I would say ahrefs would be the second most thing that I would probably get. And then I would go with hotjar and build it out from there.

You don't have to have these all right. Now. It would actually be overwhelming to get them all. Know that as we go through this training, you're going to notice that we're using a lot of these tools to explain things and show examples and we'll be digging in. So you may want to have your own accounts and the links are on this page that you can go through and sign up for things. And again, we may make a commission. It's nothing major, not life-changing money, but we may make a commission off of those. We just want to disclose that to you.

We look forward to seeing you in the next video.

FINDING TALENT (LESSON TRANSCRIPT - PLEASE PARDON GRAMMATICAL AND SPELLING ERRORS)

Hey, it's Dave back again. And right now, we're gonna talk about finding talent. There is a very strong possibility that you don't have a programmer and a writer and a designer and a video person and an organizer and a link builder and a paid traffic specialist right there on your team.

If you do, that's great, because you'll be able to quickly organize those people and get things done. But we've found over the years some solutions that really work well for us when it comes to finding talent for our projects.

The first I want to go over is Upwork.

The neat thing about Upwork is when you go to search for something like "infographic designer," just as an example, you can look at people who have successfully created infographics and see their success rates on jobs, how much they've earned, and what they make per hour. You can see this person has 92 percent job success. And then when you dig in a little bit more, you can see the work that they've done and the feedback that they've received. So here's someone who said 3.9 is their rating. You know, you can look in and actually see why. Generally speaking, people that command much higher dollar amounts per hour are the ones who are successfully doing work on Upwork and are really successful in what they do.

You can find programmers; you can find motion graphics developers who are pretty difficult sometimes to find. So you can find just about anything here on Upwork. And again, we just always recommend that you look for people that have earned a significant amount of money and have one hundred percent job success, or maybe you'll be into somebody with, for example, this ninety-five percenter. I would probably, look at him as well.

The important thing is that you do a very in-depth design brief. You want to tell a story in this design brief of what the user is going to experience. So if you're building a tool, for example, you would create an outline of what the person using the tool would experience. Then I'm going to show you a tool called Lucid Chart in just a moment where you can take that experience and put some visuals around it. It's very important to do that brief if you don't do the brief and explain things in detail, you can't expect to get a quality product back that you like.

There's another thing I highly recommend when you use a service like Upwork or word agents, which is what I'm going to show you in a moment. It's really important to check on things as they go. Don't drop the project in someone's lap and then not communicate with them for four weeks until you expect it to be done. Do checkups regularly so that you can make sure the project is on task in the way that you want it to be.

Creating an account on Upwork is easy. It's just a simple sign up and you go through and you're on your way. You can do just about anything. You see at the top here, these categories, you've got web development and these are full stack developers. You've got mobile development for apps and things, design for logos, writing, admin support, customer service, marketing, accounting. There are a lot of different things here where you can hire professionals and have a team of people ready to rock and roll on your ProfitPath®.

The next is Word Agents.

When it comes to creating really good, in-depth, lengthy content, we've had an incredible amount of success using word agents. Brian Rossiter is our internal content writer, but he has access to use writers for different areas and different expertise. This is one of the ones that he uses. Again, though, it's really important to make sure that you have a really solid design brief when you launch your campaign to hire writers because if they don't understand exactly what you need them to do, they're not going to be able to do it effectively. A lot of us, I think, go through life and our business and we assume that other people understand what we understand. We speak from a place of the knowledge that we already have in our minds. So it's difficult sometimes to express that to people in a way that they can understand it without that background knowledge that we've subconsciously built up in our minds through the years.

From a design perspective, 99designs is great.

Design does not mean web development. A lot of people confuse web design or designing an app with graphic design. Design is for things like creating a look for a Web site, but they're not going to code it necessarily. Some of them do as an additional service. But 99Designs is great for things like product logos, boxes, book covers, things like that. I actually had my book cover done through 99designs. What's neat about it is: you post a design brief and then you have sometimes hundreds of different designers from around the globe that design pieces for you to look at and then you select semifinalists and then finalists and then you select a winner. You only pay when you actually get a design that you love.

You'll find 99designs to be a little more expensive than other places on the internet, but we've personally found their quality to be really, really solid.

This is an article that I found on how to write a design brief that will keep your Web projects on track, and it has a really solid breakdown of what exactly you should include within the design brief. Things like:.

- Who's your target audience?
- What are the design requirements?
- Is there a schedule?

It's really important when you're designing something for 19-year-old females compared to sixty-five year old males, that your products have a completely different look and feel and this will break it down.

This is a tool called MindMup that we use.

It's included within Google Drive. There are paid versions as well. We use this to break out our stuff, so to speak. We will create a map that looks something like what you're looking at here that breaks out what something is going to look like in the end. We design it and lay it out like this. It helps the designer and the developer to work together to understand how something's actually going to work. So this is the main home screen and the login screen. This was obviously for a tool that we created. Then what we do is we break down those and put specific things like what's going to happen when somebody lands on this tool. What's going to happen when they press this button? Things like that. And we break it all out in here. Then you have a written map so that you can communicate effectively with the people you're bringing into the project to make it all happen.

Another great resource, if you're a little more DIY, do it yourself is Envato.

They have a bunch of different brands. Envato studio where you can hire designers similar to Upwork. Envato Elements has a bunch of creative assets like high-end clip art and stuff like that. Placeit is where you can create mockups and things. You've got the market where you have all these digital assets, tutorials on how to do specific things, and then also Envato sites, which we don't necessarily recommend, but it is there as well. One of the Envato things that we use a lot is Theme Forest. Themeforest is the market to go to get video and audio and graphics and photos and 3D files. So if we go to code, for example, to get some kind of CSS animation for something that we're gonna be doing, you can actually download different CSS animations and you can sort by best rated so that when you see these different effects, you can see how they're rated by people on the web that have used them in the past.

We also encourage our programmers and our designers to use tools like this to get started on projects. Now, they always put their customization to it, but in the beginning, it's nice sometimes to have a starting point to code from because most of the things that are in this list are items that can be modified and changed and whatnot.

So these are some tools that you can use to find people to help you with your projects. I don't think there's any ProfitPath® we've ever created where there weren't people available on Upwork or otherwise. So if you wanted paid LinkedIn traffic, for example, we can type in "paid linked in traffic". (And I'm doing this for the first time). You can see these are people that have some kind of paid LinkedIn traffic mentioned inside of their profile. So that can help you. If you see somebody that's earned over 100k that has a 99% job success rate, that is a really, really,

really good sign that they are doing amazing work for people. This person has earned almost a million dollars at $95 an hour. And, you know. So if you're doing a campaign where you want to send paid traffic to an asset, that could be a great person. Here are LinkedIn and Instagram. Now, remember, all these people come up because somewhere they put the word LinkedIn in their profile so you could have them work with you there.

One of the things I recommend is that you create a brief, put it online, and then go into Upwork and hand-select people and invite them to your brief – your job, because then you're not going to have to deal with the people who aren't as high quality and are just trying to get started. If you're looking to do serious business stuff, it's not the best decision in most cases to give a lot of people their first shot at making it, so to speak.

So I hope this helps you to learn where to find people that you can hire to do your ProfitPaths®. We look forward to seeing you in not the next lesson, but the next course, because this is the final course of the overview of ProfitPaths®. And we want you to take the test as well. The quiz that's up next. So feel free to do that and we'll see what you remember and how much you retained.

FOR NOW, THAT'S WHAT I HAVE TO SAY ABOUT THAT.

By the time you pick up this book, it's guaranteed to be outdated. The reality is that strategies, algorithms, tools, and networks change. This fact alone is what made this book an effort that took more than 10 years (not exaggerating) to complete.

Finally, I just felt like I was providing a disservice to its potential readers and pushed myself to make it happen.

I'm not sure if I will be writing more or not. If you want more, let me know. My email is daveconklin@gmail.com, and you can find me @davidalanco on Instagram.

My goal was to provide one book that would allow you to pick my brain. I hope I did that. I hope that you're able to take a lot of what's here and work with your team to implement strategies that enable you to celebrate with huge ROI gains.

I'll end with a few "dad jokes," as they have become my favorite way to embarrass my kids when they're around their friends.

Q: How do billboards talk?

A: Sign Language

That's a good one. I don't care who ya' are.

Thanks for hanging with me,

Dave

ACKNOWLEDGEMENTS

My career wouldn't be where it is without so many people, but without Christ, it wouldn't exist at all. I've made many mistakes in my life and handled things in ways that I'm embarrassed about like the rest of us. I don't deserve this awesome life I live, and it's only because of His grace that I'm here. The best advice I could give to anyone is to get plugged into a life-giving church and really dig into what Jesus is all about. That advice will take you light years ahead of the advice in this book will.

My wife, Jodi, is amazing. There have been so many times when she dealt with things at home while I traveled to business events to speak or worked late at night. She's also had my back in such a huge way long before I was even a marketer. She's the most influential force in my life and has made me a better person. I'm proud she picked me, even after we've been together for almost 20 years. Thanks for continuing to inspire me, "Jod."

My parents have built me up to be a person who has a sense of confidence that doesn't make sense. I'm so grateful to them for pouring into me. My mom said once when I was a kid in the car, "would you like to see your name in lights?" I don't actually remember what I said, but I hope to have fulfilled her desire for me. As we get older, I think many of us appreciate our parents more and more. I'm definitely in appreciation mode.

My kids, Emily, Haley, Matt, and Marc: thank you so much for the laughter, the support, the pride and the unintentional accountability you've given me. It's an amazing feeling when some of the people you would choose to spend the most time with are your kids, and it's not out of parental obligation.

My past and current business partners: Steve Young, Josh Eberly, Matt Self, Steve Foley, Rory Wilfong, Patrick Miller, Randy Wenger, and some unnamed, thank you for believing in my crazy ideas. We have had so much fun together and there's a lot more to come.

To the thousands of people who have seen me speak and the hundreds of business owners I've had the opportunity to help directly, I don't know why you trusted me, but you did - and I hope I can continue to help more and more for years to come.

"Risking Nothing Is Risking Even More."

- Too Many To Source